kitchen seasons

kitchen seasons

easy recipes for seasonal organic food

Ross Dobson

photography by Richard Jung

RYLAND
PETERS
& SMALL

LONDON NEW YORK

Dedication
This book is dedicated to those who
do all the hard work to bring us fantastic
food. To the market farmers, providers,
and growers who are up much earlier
in the morning than most of us could
imagine, in rain, hail, or shine. You are
very much appreciated.

Design and Photographic Art Direction
  Steve Painter
Editors Julia Charles and Ann Baggaley
Production Manager Patricia Harrington
Publishing Director Alison Starling

Food Stylist Ross Dobson
Prop Stylist Róisín Nield

Indexer Hilary Bird

First published in the USA in 2007
by Ryland Peters & Small, Inc.
519 Broadway, 5th Floor
New York, NY 10012
www.rylandpeters.com

10 9 8 7 6 5 4 3 2 1

Printed and bound in China

Library of Congress Cataloging-in-
Publication Data

Dobson, Ross, 1965-
  Kitchen seasons : easy recipes for
seasonal organic food / Ross Dobson.
    p. cm.
  Includes index.
  ISBN 978-1-84597-467-1
1. Cookery (Natural foods) 2. Quick and
easy cookery. I. Title.
  TX741.D62 2007
  641.5'63--dc22

                          2007012607

Notes

• All spoon measurements are level
unless otherwise stated.

• Eggs are large unless otherwise
specified. Uncooked or partially cooked
eggs should not be served to the very
old, frail, young children, pregnant
women, or those with compromised
immune systems.

Author's Acknowledgments

A great big thank you to the crew at
Ryland, Peters & Small. To Alison, who
saw this as an idea worth pursuing and
making it possible to create this beautiful
book. To some good mates I made
during the shoot. For your beautiful
photography, Richard Jung and your
laconic wit. Are you sure you aren't
Australian? To the irrepressibly worrisome
Steve Painter, art director extraordinaire,
for your irreproachable attention to detail
and for reintroducing me to chocolate
addiction. Thanks to Jules who helped
us out at the shoot and to Ann and Julia,
back in the office, doing the hard yards
on the text. Very much appreciated.
Thank you all so much.

thoughtful food

Although today's globalized food market ensures that most of our food can be bought all year round, it is my belief that there is more pleasure to be gained in eating according to what is seasonally available. It is a simple fact that food tastes better in season and especially so when it is locally-grown or reared using organic farming methods. This book is about buying and cooking the best food and using produce that has been grown and marketed locally.

Our awareness and understanding of the seasons of food have diminished rapidly over the last few decades. This is largely due to the many large supermarket chains that offer aisle upon aisle of goods and give us an almost overwhelming choice. Sadly though, it's a merchandising strategy that seems to be based on size and uniformity of display rather than the quality and flavor of the actual foods themselves. Choice should be a positive thing but in recent years it may have become a poisoned chalice as far as good food is concerned. I cook for a living so naturally that involves an awful lot of food shopping. Supermarkets may offer us a seemingly

endless array of products all year round, making us feel like we are in complete control, but I have learned from experience that choice and convenience rarely equate to quality. The idea that we can eat what we want, when we want to initally seems liberating but at the same time we have stopped asking ourselves what we are eating and that is an important question. The amount of money we spend on food is also interesting. What is striking is that, in real terms, food has actually become cheaper, with many households now spending less on the average weekly food bill than they did twenty or thirty years ago. At the same time, we are spending more money on things that didn't exist in previous decades, such as cell phones and home computers. Unfortunately, it is bad food that is cheap to produce and while many of us don't think twice when buying the latest cell phone we may balk at paying more than we feel we have to for food. It's important to understand that paying slightly more for good, healthy food is never a false economy—you will get what you pay for and appreciate the difference it makes.

The most obvious problem with buying fruit and vegetables from supermarkets during the months when they do not grow locally is that they have to travel long distances to reach the shelves. This inevitably means that they are picked early before being given the opportunity to ripen naturally. Added to which, refrigerated transport and high-technology food storage actually prevent them from ripening, literally arresting their natural development. Not surprisingly, the end result of this is disappointing produce, totally lacking in flavor. The mighty tomato is a prime example. It doesn't actually need brilliant sunshine and rich soil in order to grow—a tomato plant is hardy and can be grown out of thin air and under artificial light! This fact has been exploited by scientists and businessmen who set out to develop a hybrid tomato that could travel long distances without bruising. The result of their labors is the mealy, tough and bland-tasting tomato you have probably eaten too many times, especially in the winter months. A tomato that has been allowed to mature naturally on the vine under the summer sunshine is something else entirely. It is a brilliant red, rich in flavour and smells exquisitely like a tomato and nothing else on earth.

Most modern supermarkets do stock organic produce of course but simply labelling something "organic" doesn't necessarily mean that it is a "good thing." For instance, many of the organic items for sale in supermarkets are imported either by air or road, which not only raises the issue of taste but also that of "food miles." Put simply, food miles are a measure of the distance a foodstuff travels from a field to your kitchen. The organic baby eggplant that you buy is highly likely to have been flown in from Thailand. Much of our food is travelling half as much again now as it did in the mid-eighties and this travel adds substantially to the carbon dioxide emissions that are generally thought to be contributing to climate change. Food miles matter and, as a consumer, by giving more thought to how far your food has travelled from plough to plate you can make a difference. In short, I truly believe that buying from your local organic farmers and markets is the best way to know what you are eating and where it has come from. Greater respect will have been paid to the natural order of the seasons and produce is more likely to have been grown with care and concern for the environment.

Besides the immediate benefits of changing the way you shop for food, such as taste, there are other longer-term ones. You'll also be supporting the local food movement. Globalization and the domination of single brands poses a threat to the distinctiveness of local culture generally, and sadly this includes food. Unique varieties of apples and potatoes are overlooked in favor of those that simply meet the bottom line. While a supermarket may offer just a few varieties of potato, a local farmers' market will have too many to list, many with exotic and sexy names like Nicola, Bintje, and Desirée and each with their own ideal culinary uses.

In addition, growers and producers are always passionate about their food. They live for it. You may even notice some of them are nuts about it! But when it comes to food, passion is always a good thing. Ask the grower for advice and I guarantee he or she will be more than happy to point you in the direction of a variety of potato that is best for your particular purpose, whether it's mashing, roasting, or using in a salad. The food you choose to buy will become personal as an alliance is formed between you and the person you are buying from. You can actually look them in the eye and ask if your potatoes of choice have been grown free of artificial fertilizers and chemical pesticides. Relax and enjoy the expert guidance and advice they offer and you will probably hear a unique story or two along the way. For instance, I recently discovered the mushrooms I had been buying for some time were all grown in the dark caverns of an abandoned Victorian railway tunnel just two hours drive from the city where I live. Could a mushroom ask for a better home in which to grow and be nurtured before making it into my kitchen? The wild garlic I often cook with comes from the oldest known crop introduced into Australia by Chinese immigrants during the gold rush of the 1800s. Knowing this, how could I ever look at a bunch of garlic in the same way again? So if you want to know more about the origin of your food, talk to your supplier and ask plenty of questions. But, be warned, if you are in a hurry it might be best to save it for another time! Doing so makes shopping for food a personal and interactive experience, something that most supermarkets could never offer. In this commercial age when everything moves at a crazy pace, it makes a welcome change when our shopping experience can be based on sound choices at the same time as being a pleasant task.

Most importantly, this book is about paying respect to the natural cycle of the seasons and the food they provide us with. We should realize that although we *can* buy most fresh produce all year round we don't *have* to do so and some things just taste better at that right time of the year. For example, a ripe summer tomato is full of flavor; strawberries picked in season have a heady, floral aroma and leeks are more silky and flavorsome in the colder months. And then there are those ingredients which seem to go hand in hand with the mood of each particular season and our appetites at that time of year—crisp young salad greens in spring, juicy and refreshing cherries in summer, musky wild mushrooms in a rich pasta sauce during fall and crisp roasted potatoes when it's cold outside.

Nature is full of these symbiotic links between the seasons and the food we eat. The seasons dictate how plants evolve and those that need cold soil in which to begin life, such as purple sprouting broccoli, are ready and bursting with goodness come the spring. Rhubarb sustains us until the fruits of summer arrive. Kale likes a good frost to give it the kick-start it needs so that it's available to give us much-needed nutrients through fall and winter. The cold, shorter days of winter are a sign for sheep to reproduce so that lambs will be born when the ground is covered with nutrient-packed grass in late spring. Traditionally, other meats were a treat reserved for the autumn and winter months. Pigs were fattened with the windfalls of autumn – rotting apples unfit for human consumption and tasty bits scavenged from the forest floor. These leftovers would be scoffed down bulking the pigs up for bacon and other cured meats to feed us through the lean winter months.

Kitchen Seasons is not intended to be the last word on seasonal cooking. Far from it. Let's hope there are many more books on the subject and that this way of approaching how we shop, cook, and eat gains in popularity and once again becomes a way of life for most people. I've developed this collection of simple, no-fuss recipes around the idea of using fresh seasonal produce when it is at its peak—mother nature has done all the hard work already! The emphasis is on simplicity without dumbing down, and partnering simple produce with other good-quality ingredients, such as cheeses, nuts, cured meats, and smoked fish. And there is no reason to be intimidated by my style of cooking—I have always championed the idea of cheating in the kitchen whenever possible in order to save time and unnecessary sweat. I use my food processor to make cakes, prefer shop-bought curry pastes to blending my own, and believe that frozen ready-made pastry is a convenient and acceptable alternative to making it yourself. I also recommend having a kitchen pantry packed full of versatile cooking staples. Stock up on basics like pasta, noodles, and polenta, rice and couscous, beans, chick peas and lentils plus a good selection of oils, vinegars, and Asian seasonings. When it comes to fresh food such as meat, dairy, and vegetables, buy it in relatively small quantities on a weekly basis.

Put simply, *Kitchen Seasons* is about making the most of food in all its glorious, seasonal prime, just as nature intended...

spring

the tastes of **spring**

The birds are becoming noisy and the bees are busy. Spring is the season when things start to happen. Even if we aren't aware of it, nature is busy doing what it does best; growing things. It seems to happen almost without us realizing but then suddenly we are no longer waking up in the dark and can enjoy a lunchtime sandwich sitting outside in the warm sunshine. By the time we have noticed it's beginning to warm up, buds have already formed on the trees, spring flowers are beginning to bloom, and the grass really is greener! You may still be feeling gray but nature is very busy getting green and as we expel our last few breaths of winter air, things in the ground are really starting to move and shake.

Spring food should be fresh and crisp. As much as we enjoyed the leeks, onions, and potatoes that sustained us through the winter months, it is now time to move on. When you shop for locally-grown organic food in spring it may seem as if pickings are slim. The many crops planted in fall that saw us through winter have all but gone and it's far too early for any summertime produce. Unsurprisingly, this time of year is known as "the hungry gap" and things may seem especially lean in April.

But take comfort because what is available is good, very good indeed. We crave "rabbit food" at this time of year and lovely young **salad greens** are at their very best. These can be bought by the bag at farmers' markets and often you can select your own from large barrels—look out for peppery little arugula leaves, mesclun, and delicate **baby spinach**.

This really is the the time of year for creative cooking and using all of your pantry goodies to breathe life into the relatively limited fresh food that's available. Rummage right to the back of your shelves and take stock of what you've got. See what can be used to whip up piquant dressings to go with smoked chicken and trout salads. Use classic Asian sauces to season simple stir-fries or to lightly pickle **tender young vegetables**.

Get over your tofu phobia and embrace its goodness, no longer reserved just for hippies. Keep bags of **golden grains** in your kitchen. Couscous and bulgur (cracked wheat) add a satisfying and earthy dimension to any spring salad. Both are inexpensive and store well. Make a basic tabbouleh, then become more adventurous and try adding some aromatic spices or toasted nuts. Lamb cutlets become truly exotic with a sprinkle or two of ground cumin and coriander. Stock your fridge with the long-life Cypriot cheese halloumi—cube it and add to a creamy spinach curry. Buy fresh and light **ricotta** cheese and use it to make a delicious baked cheesecake to serve with tangy poached **rhubarb**. Spring may not be a season when fruit is available in abundance but rhubarb is at its peak and there to be enjoyed.

Asparagus is in its glorious prime in springtime too. Steamed, stir-fried, or simply blanched to an emerald green and tossed into fresh pasta—it is always a seasonal treat. For something really special, try it pan-fried in butter and combined with creamy and tangy goat cheese on a buttery puff pastry base.

Purple sprouting broccoli is another cause for celebration—it is a bit of a tart as it goes with just about anything! It willingly partners typical Asian flavors and is delicious in a vegetable stir-fry with just a splash of soy sauce, sesame oil, and garlic. It works just as well with pasta and freshly grated Parmesan cheese, toasted pine nuts, and pepper flakes, and a drizzle of fruity olive oil.

Highly nutritious, but lighter and fresher tasting than other cabbages, **spring greens** are yet another treat. Lightly steamed and tossed in a rich lemony butter, they are an ideal side to fish cakes made with rich and indulgent wild salmon and the old-fashioned herb sorrel.

Meat and poultry follow a natural cycle throughout the seasons too, something we can easily forget in these modern days of all-year-round supplies of pork and beef. **Lamb** is tender and tasty now and **spring chickens** are even more succulent when roasted with an Italian-style herbed ricotta and lemon stuffing.

pickled spring vegetable and marinated tofu salad

You will usually see tofu sold as soft and firm but you may also be able to buy a dark, pressed, marinated tofu. If you can't find it, it's easy enough to flavor your own with soy sauce and Chinese five-spice powder. Its creamy, mildy spiced and salty flavour goes very well with lightly-pickled spring vegetables. The vegetables are not pickled in the old-fashioned way, which leaves them limp, but kept fresh and crisp, just how mother nature intended.

12 sugar snap peas
12 snow peas, cut in half
1 bunch of asparagus, trimmed and halved
2 tablespoons sugar
⅓ cup rice vinegar (or balsamic vinegar)
1 small daikon (white radish), cut into julienne strips
6–8 scallions, thinly sliced on the angle
1 small bunch of fresh cilantro, chopped
3 tablespoons light soy sauce
½ teaspoon sesame oil
1 tablespoon sesame seeds, lightly toasted (optional)

marinated tofu:
3 tablespoons light soy sauce
½ teaspoon Chinese five-spice powder
20 oz. block firm tofu

Serves 4

For the marinated tofu, put the soy sauce and five-spice powder in a bowl large enough to snugly fit the block of tofu. Add the tofu to the bowl and toss around to coat in the marinade. Cover with plastic wrap and refrigerate for a minimum of 3 hours or overnight, turning often. Drain well and slice the tofu into thin batons.

Bring a saucepan of lightly salted water to the boil and add the sugar snaps, snow peas and asparagus and blanche in the hot water for 1 minute. Drain and place in a large bowl of ice water until completely cold. Drain well and put into another bowl.

Put the sugar and vinegar in small saucepan and boil for 5 minutes, until thickened slightly. Remove from the heat and let cool. Pour the vinegar mix over the blanched vegetables and daikon, stir well and set aside for 30 minutes. Add the scallions, cilantro and tofu to the pickled vegetables, gently tossing to combine. Mix the soy sauce and sesame oil in a small bowl and pour over the salad. Toss gently, then transfer to a serving dish and sprinkle the sesame seeds over the top.

potato and smoked trout salad with dill and cashew pesto

Little new potatoes are perfect for salads. Their skins are still young and haven't set which makes them easy to peel after boiling. But why bother? They are so sweet and taste just fine boiled with the skins left on and tossed with a little butter. This version of a pesto is divine and can be used as a condiment to any grilled fish or chicken dish or, as it is here, with a salad of potatoes, smoked trout and spinach.

16 small new potatoes
1 smoked trout, flesh flaked
1 lb. baby spinach
lemon wedges, to serve

dill and cashew pesto:
½ cup unsalted cashews, lightly toasted
2 tablespoons snipped fresh dill
a handful of flatleaf parsley, roughly chopped
1 tablespoon freshly squeezed lemon juice
1 garlic clove, chopped
¼ cup extra virgin olive oil
2 tablespoons finely grated Parmesan cheese
sea salt and freshly ground black pepper

Serves 4

To make the pesto, put the cashews, herbs, lemon juice, garlic and olive oil in a food processor and process to form a rough paste. Remove to a bowl and stir in the Parmesan. Season to taste with salt and black pepper and set aside.

Put the potatoes in a saucepan and cover with cold water. Cook over high heat and as soon as the water boils, remove the pan from the heat, cover the pan with a tight-fitting lid and leave for 20 minutes. Drain the potatoes, slice them in half and put them in a large bowl. Add the trout and the spinach and gently toss to mix. You can either add the pesto and gently toss the salad to coat it in the dressing or, if you prefer the fish not to break up too much, serve the pesto on the side.

Serve with lemon wedges to squeeze over.

See photograph on page 14.

smoked chicken, apple, and radish salad

My local tapas bar does a wonderful radish and apple salad but true to authentic tapas style it is a small serving and I am always left wanting more. So when I make my own version I beef it up with the addition of smoked chicken and almonds. These flavors go so well together. I use a late apple variety, like Pink Lady, which are still crisp and fresh going into the early days of spring but if you have trouble getting these add some extra spinach or crispy blanched snow peas as a substitute.

2 smoked chicken breasts, shredded
½ cup smoked almonds, roughly chopped
2 apples, cored and thinly sliced
2 large red radishes, sliced into thin discs
4 white anchovies, roughly chopped
3½ oz. baby spinach
½ cup mayonnaise
1 tablespoon finely chopped chervil
2 tablespoons freshly squeezed lemon juice

Serves 4

Put the chicken in a large bowl with the almonds, apple, radish, anchovies and spinach. Gently toss to evenly mix, then transfer to a serving plate.

Put the mayonnaise, chervil and lemon juice in a bowl and mix well. Serve on the side.

Next time: Substitute the chicken for 16 large cooked shrimp that have been shelled and deveined or add a handful of seedless grapes and some blanched snow peas.

See photograph on page 15.

chicken, avocado, and mesclun salad

Mesclun is at its peak in spring. Perfect timing for when the craving sets in for something fresh and light or, as some people like to call it, "rabbit food." The mesclun in this salad can be replaced with any mixture of young, tender salad greens, such as rocket, frisée or radicchio leaves. Any variety with a peppery bite will work with the chicken, buttery avocados and liquoricy basil.

2 organic chicken breasts, skin on
1 tablespoon light olive oil
⅔ cup mayonnaise
6–8 large basil leaves, roughly torn
1 teaspoon Dijon mustard
8 small handfuls of mesclun
2 firm avocados
1 small red onion, thinly sliced
sea salt

Serves 4

Preheat the oven to 350°F. Rub sea salt over the skin of the chicken breasts. Heat the oil in a nonstick frying pan over high heat and cook the chicken breasts, skin side-down, for 2 minutes. Turn over and cook for a further 2 minutes, then transfer the chicken to a roasting pan and cook in the preheated oven for 10 minutes. Remove, cover with aluminium foil and set aside while you prepare the rest of the salad.

Put the mayonnaise, basil and mustard in a food processor and process for about 10 seconds.

Arrange the mesclun on a flat serving platter. Slice the chicken against the grain into thick strips and arrange over the salad. Cut the avocados in half and remove the stone. Use a large metal spoon to scoop out the flesh. Thinly slice the avocado and arrange over the chicken. Scatter the sliced onion on top. Dollop the dressing over the salad or serve the salad in individual portions with the dressing on the side.

Next time: Try this salad served in warmed pita bread or wrapped burrito-style in soft flour tortillas.

It's fun to hand pick salad greens, making up your own mix. You will find big barrels or bags of lovely tender spring salad greens at your local market. When buying greens, keep in mind you will need about two large handfuls per person. Avoid limp looking greens. If they do wilt a little on the way home on warmer days, give them a quick bath in a bowl of cold water with a pinch or two of sugar thrown in. This will freshen them up. The spring fresh ingredients are combined here with bulgur. This is cracked wheat and may be one of man's first attempts at processing food. Simply cover with boiling water to soften and add to your favorite salad ingredients.

tabbouleh with chickpeas and spring salad

½ cup fine bulgur (cracked wheat)

2 tablespoons freshly squeezed lemon juice

¼ cup extra virgin olive oil

1 small bunch of flatleaf parsley, finely chopped

1 large handful of mint leaves, finely chopped

2 tablespoons finely snipped dill

1 small basket of cherry tomatoes, halved

14 oz. canned chickpeas, rinsed and drained

4–5 oz. spring salad mix

sea salt and freshly ground black pepper

toasted flatbread, to serve (optional)

Serves 4

Put the bulgur in a heatproof bowl and pour over ½ cup boiling water. Stir once, cover tightly with plastic wrap and set aside for 8–10 minutes. Put the lemon juice and olive oil in a small bowl and whisk. Pour over the bulgur and stir well with a fork, fluffing up the bulgur and separating the grains.

Put the bulgur in a large bowl with the parsley, mint, dill, tomatoes, chickpeas, and salad greens. Use your hands to toss everything together. Season well with sea salt and black pepper. Transfer to a serving plate and serve with toasted flatbread, if you like.

Next time: Try serving this salad alongside the Spiced Lamb Cutlets on page 39 or the Prosciutto-wrapped Fish on page 32.

asparagus and goat cheese tart

2 x 12-oz. sheets ready-rolled puff pastry dough, defrosted if frozen

1 egg, lightly beaten and mixed with 2 teaspoons water

2 tablespoons butter

2 tablespoons light olive oil

2 bunches thin asparagus, woody ends trimmed

5 oz. soft goat cheese

sea salt and freshly ground black pepper

2 baking sheets, lined with baking paper

Serves 4, as a starter

Beautiful, fresh, young asparagus will be easy to bend without snapping and require little or next to no cooking time. There's no need to cut the woody ends off either— gently bend the ends and they will naturally snap at the right point. Asparagus doesn't store or freeze well so there's even more reason to buy your bunch from a farmers' market so that you can be sure it has been picked fresh. In spring, buying fresh asparagus won't be difficult at all.

Preheat the oven to 425°F. Cut the sheets of pastry to make two rectangles 10 x 5 inches and place each one on a baking sheet lined with parchment paper. Cut ½ inch wide strips from the remaining pastry. Brush around the edges of the pastry rectangles and place the strips on the edges to form a border. Prick the centre of each pastry with a fork and brush the beaten egg all over it. Cook in the preheated oven for 15 minutes, until pale golden and puffed.

Put the butter and olive oil in a frying pan over high heat and cook the asparagus for 2–3 minutes, turning often, until just beginning to soften. Season well with sea salt and black pepper and set aside. Crumble the goat cheese over the pastry, staying within the borders. Top with the asparagus and cook in the oven for a further 10 minutes until the pastry is dark golden. Serve warm.

This history of this exotic soup can be traced back to the colonial influences of the French in Vietnam. The clear stock is similar to a *consommé*. It is known as a *pho* in Vietnam, named after the rice noodles used in the soup. It all sounds very exotic, doesn't it? But all you need is a lovely young, organic chicken, some fresh spring herbs, and a visit to your local speciality Asian store. Dead simple and so full of the fresh flavors of spring. I like to use Thai basil when I can but don't stress if this is hard to find. It's the aniseed flavor of basil you need here so any variety will do just as well.

spring chicken soup with rice noodles and herbs

1 small organic spring chicken, weighing about 2¼–2½ lbs.

2 star anise

1 cinnamon stick

2 tablespoons Thai fish sauce, plus extra for seasoning

6½ oz. rice stick noodles, about ½ inch wide

1 large handful of fresh mint leaves

1 handful of fresh basil (ideally Thai) leaves, torn

1 large handful of cilantro leaves

1 cup bean sprouts

2 limes, cut into wedges

Serves 4

Wash the chicken well. Put the chicken in a large saucepan and cover with 3 quarts cold water. Add the star anise and cinnamon to the pan and put over high heat. Bring the water to a boil, reduce the heat to low and simmer for 15 minutes. Cover the pan with a tight-fitting lid, remove from the heat and let the chicken poach for 1 hour. Remove the chicken from the pan and pour 2 quarts of the stock into a clean saucepan (keep the remaining stock for later use.) Add the fish sauce to the stock and simmer over low heat. When the chicken is cool enough to handle shred the meat, discarding the skin and bones.

Put the noodles in a heatproof bowl, cover with boiling water and let stand for 10 minutes, or until soft. Drain well and divide between 4 serving bowls. Top with the chicken and ladle over the hot broth. Top each soup with some herbs and bean sprouts and serve with fresh lime wedges on the side to squeeze over and some fish sauce to season.

Next time: The flesh of poached chicken is soft and succulent which makes it perfect for throwing in a salad or a light Thai or Indian curry.

pasta with purple sprouting broccoli, chiles, and pine nuts

Purple sprouting broccoli is the sweeter, tender younger brother to the other more common and chunky members of the brassica family. Typically in season early spring, you may be lucky enough to see it as early as Christmas in more temperate climates. Either way, its appearance causes much excitement after what seems like months of winter vegetables. A long-awaited seasonal treat, the purple sprouting broccoli is used here in the simplest of pasta dishes to make perfect supper fare. Remember it's the chile seeds that carry the heat, so if you like things spicy, leave the seeds in one, or both, of the chiles.

14 oz. orecchiette pasta, or similar
14 oz. purple sprouting broccoli,
roughly chopped
3 tablespoons butter
2 tablespoons light olive oil
2 small red chiles, deseeded and
finely chopped
2 garlic cloves, thinly sliced
¼ cup pine nuts
1 cup finely grated Parmesan cheese

Serves 4

Cook the pasta according to the packet instructions. Drain well and return to the warm pan.

Cook the broccoli pieces in salted boiling water for 2 minutes and drain well.

Heat the butter and oil in a frying pan over medium heat. When the butter is sizzling, add the chiles, garlic, and pine nuts and cook for 3–4 minutes, stirring often, until the garlic has softened and the pine nuts are starting to turn golden. Add the broccoli and stir to coat in the other ingredients. Add the broccoli mixture to the pasta with half of the Parmesan and stir well. Serve with the remaining cheese served on the side to sprinkle over the pasta.

asparagus tagliatelle

Young asparagus is one of life's great gifts. Because it is such a treat, keep it simple. Of course it is wonderful blanched and served with hollandaise but this is a perfect pasta starter, combining the prime spears with a handful of other fresh, good-quality ingredients.

1 cup light cream
10 oz. tagliatelle pasta, or simliar
1 bunch of fine asparagus, trimmed and each spear cut into 4
grated zest and freshly squeezed juice of
1 unwaxed lemon
3 tablespoons finely chopped flatleaf parsley
1 cup finely grated Parmesan cheese
sea salt and freshly ground black pepper

Serves 4, as a starter

Put the cream in a small saucepan and bring to a boil. Reduce the heat to a low simmer and cook for 8–10 minutes, until slightly thickened. Set aside.

Cook the pasta according to the packet instructions. About 2 minutes before the pasta is cooked, add the asparagus to the boiling water. Drain well and return to the warm pan with the reduced cream, lemon zest and juice, parsley and half of the Parmesan. Toss together, season well with sea salt and black pepper and serve with the remaining cheese sprinkled on top.

Next time: As a substitute to asparagus, pan-fry 1 grated small zucchini in 1 tablespoon of butter over medium heat until softened and golden. Add the zucchini to the well-drained pasta along with the other ingredients.

This stir-fry is very fresh and very Thai in its simplicity and balance of flavors. Although soft tofu runs the risk of breaking up, it's preferable to the firm variety as its creamier, more silky texture goes well with crispy spring vegetables. You will only need to quickly cook the greens in boiling water to soften them a little, and this also brings out their brilliant emerald green. The mushrooms, available from any speciality Asian store, are one of my favorite pantry secrets—they are inexpensive and will keep indefinitely stored in a container. My tip of putting the tofu on paper towels is one you can use for other recipes using soft tofu and is especially good for fried tofu dishes.

stir-fried tofu with crisp greens and mushrooms

10 oz. soft tofu, cut into 1-inch cubes

8 dried Chinese mushrooms

2 garlic cloves

2 oz. sugar snap peas, trimmed

2 oz. snow peas, trimmed

2 bunches of fine asparagus, cut into 2-inch lengths

¼ cup vegetable or light peanut oil

1 tablespoon light soy sauce

a pinch of sugar

a pinch of ground white pepper

sea salt

steamed jasmine rice, to serve (optional)

Serves 4

Put the tofu on several layers of paper towel and leave for 20–30 minutes to absorb excess moisture. Put the mushrooms in a heatproof bowl and cover with boiling water. Set aside for 20 minutes. Drain the mushrooms, remove the stems and halve any larger ones.

Put the garlic in a mortar with a good pinch of sea salt and pound to a paste.

Cook the vegetables in boiling water for 30 seconds, until bright emerald green in colour and softened. Rinse well under cold water until completely cold.

Heat a wok over high heat, then add the oil. Cook the tofu cubes in the hot oil for 5 minutes, turning often, until light golden and puffed. Transfer the tofu to paper towel and pour off all but 2 tablespoons of oil from the wok. Add the vegetables to the wok and stir-fry for 2 minutes. Add the mushrooms and gently stir-fry for 1 minute. Add the garlic paste and stir-fry for 1 minute, then add the soy sauce, a pinch of white pepper, a pinch of sugar and 2 tablespoons water to the wok. Return the tofu to the wok and stir-fry gently for 1 minute to coat all the ingredients in the sauce, being careful not to break up the tofu. Remove the wok from the heat and serve with steamed jasmine rice, if you like.

I am a big fan of Indian vegetarian cooking and after a really good Indian meal I am often tempted to race home to make some of the fantastic dishes I have eaten. I was always especially intimidated at the thought of making my own *palak paneer*, a spinach and cheese curry, but then I had a go. It wasn't too difficult at all and I was more than impressed with the results. Paneer is a firm, fresh white Indian cheese. It's not that easy to find and I discovered that halloumi, a cheese from Cyprus, will do the trick. The other ingredients are all readily available—fresh spring spinach and a good-quality curry paste. I do recommend cheating and using pre-made curry pastes. They keep well in the refrigerator and save you from having a cupboard full of dry spices that have a short shelf life.

spinach and cheese curry

1 tablespoon vegetable oil

8 oz. paneer or halloumi, cut into 1-inch cubes

2 tablespoons butter

2 tablespoons mild Indian curry paste (Madras or balti)

2 large green chiles (optional), deseeded and chopped

1 lb. spinach, roughly chopped

a handful of chopped fresh cilantro, leaves and stems

½ cup light cream

lemon wedges, to garnish

basmati rice and warm naan bread, to serve (optional)

Serves 4

Heat the oil in a nonstick frying pan over high heat and cook the cubes of cheese for 2–3 minutes, turning often, until golden all over. Remove the cheese to a plate and set aside until needed.

Add the butter to the pan and when sizzling hot, add the curry paste and green chiles and stir-fry for 2 minutes. Add the spinach and cilantro and cook for 3–4 minutes, until all the spinach has wilted, then stir in the cream.

Put the mixture in a food processor and process until the sauce is thick and smooth. Return to the pan, add the cheese and cook over low heat for 2–3 minutes, to warm the cheese through.

Serve the curry spooned over basmati rice with warm naan bread on the side, if you like.

Wild salmon is not an inexpensive fish but it is a true seasonal treat. It isn't available year round, unlike the farmed salmon, which are not entirely unremarkable in the impact they have on local ecosystems and the amount of resources they consume. Remember, wild salmon will have a natural powder pink salmon hue, not the blazing orange color of farmed fish. Sorrel is a terribly old-fashioned herb, coming into season when little else does. Its lemony bite makes it a perfect partner for wild spring salmon and of course the highly nutritious side of collard greens is an essential accompaniment.

wild salmon and sorrel cakes with buttered collard greens

2 fresh bay leaves

2 cups whole milk

1 lb. wild salmon

3 medium potatoes (about 20 oz.), quartered

6–8 large sorrel leaves, thinly sliced
or 1 teaspoon lemon thyme leaves

1 egg, lightly beaten

4 scallions, chopped

2½ cups fresh breadcrumbs

¼ cup light olive oil

1 bunch of spring greens, thickly sliced

2 tablespoons butter

2 tablespoons freshly squeezed lemon juice

sea salt and freshly ground black pepper

lemon wedges, to serve (optional)

Serves 4

Put the bay leaves and milk in a small frying pan and bring to simmering point. Add the salmon, turn off the heat, and let the salmon poach for 5 minutes. Remove the salmon and discard the poaching liquid. When the salmon is cool enough to handle, gently flake the flesh and place it in a bowl.

Cook the potatoes in a saucepan of boiling water for 10 minutes. Drain and roughly mash them. Let cool to room temperature. Put the mashed potatoes in the bowl with the salmon and add the sorrel, egg, scallions, and ¾ cup of the breadcrumbs. Season well with sea salt and black pepper. Using your hands, form the mixture into 8 large patties.

Put the remaining breadcrumbs in a bowl and gently roll the fish cakes in the crumbs to evenly coat all over. Put the fish cakes on a plate, cover and refrigerate until needed.

Heat the oil in a nonstick frying pan over medium heat and cook the fish cakes for 3–4 minutes on each side, until the crumbs are cooked and golden.

Meanwhile, cook the collard greens in a saucepan of boiling water for 5 minutes. Drain well. Add the butter and lemon juice to the warm pan and stir well. Return the greens to the pan, season with sea salt and toss to coat in the lemony butter.

Spoon the greens onto serving plates and top with the fish cakes. Serve with lemon wedges for squeezing over the fish cakes, if you like.

I have used a snapper fillet from my local supplier but go ahead and use a similar weight and cut of any firm white fish, preferably from a sustainable fishery. I know, these tart little cherry tomatoes are really a summer thing, but towards the warmer days of late spring, who can resist? For the pesto we have a simple twist on the classic, replacing the traditional pine nuts with walnuts which are combined with the most wonderfully fresh spring herbs.

prosciutto-wrapped fish with walnut pesto and balsamic tomatoes

3 tablespoons extra virgin olive oil
24 cherry tomatoes
1 tablespoon balsamic vinegar
4 slices of prosciutto or Parma ham
4 white fish cutlets, of 200 g each
sea salt and freshly ground black pepper

walnut pesto:
1 handful of flatleaf parsley leaves
1 handful of mint leaves
2 handfuls of basil leaves
2 tablespoons snipped fresh dill
¾ cup walnuts
1 garlic clove, crushed
⅔ cup light olive oil
½ cup finely grated Parmesan cheese

Serves 4

To make the walnut pesto, put the herbs, walnuts, garlic, and olive oil in a food processor and process until chunky. Transfer to a bowl and stir in the Parmesan. Season to taste with sea salt and black pepper. Cover and refrigerate until needed.

Put 2 tablespoons of the olive oil in a nonstick frying pan over high heat and add the tomatoes. Cook for 2–3 minutes, shaking the pan. Add the balsamic vinegar to the pan with some sea salt and black pepper, cover with a lid and shake the pan over high heat for 1 minute, until the tomatoes soften and start to split.

Remove the tomatoes and wipe the pan clean. Wrap a slice of prosciutto around the centre of each fish fillet. Add the remaining oil to the pan and cook the fish fillets for 2–3 minutes on each side, until the prosciutto is golden and crispy.

Serve the fish with the balsamic tomatoes and spoon the pesto on the side.

An organic farmer once said that for a chicken to truly taste like a chicken, it must have lived like a chicken and this made a lot of sense to me. Buying your bird at a farmers' market is the very best way to guarantee the quality. Many stalls will provide brochures or have a website showing where the animal has come from so that you can be sure it had a good home before it made it into your kitchen. Rubbing the herb and ricotta mixture between the skin and meat keeps the flesh moist and ensures the whole bird stays succulent. It may seem over indulgent to roast a chicken with cheese but ricotta is surprisingly low in fat. Ricotta seems like such an indulgence but it really isn't, which is why I am such a big fan.

roasted spring chicken with herbs and ricotta

8 oz. ricotta cheese

2 tablespoons finely chopped fresh basil

3 tablespoons finely chopped flatleaf parsley leaves

2 garlic cloves, chopped

2 tablespoons light olive oil

1 teaspoon sea salt

grated zest and freshly squeezed juice of 1 unwaxed lemon

1 organic chicken, weighing about 2½ lbs.

2 lemons, cut in half

kitchen string

Serves 2

Preheat the oven to 350°F.

Put the ricotta in a bowl with the basil, parsley, garlic, 1 tablespoon of the olive oil, sea salt, lemon juice, and zest and mix well.

Wash and dry the chicken with paper towels. Use your hands to carefully separate the skin from the meat, without tearing the skin, and force the ricotta mixture between the skin and the meat. Rub the extra cut lemon halves over the chicken then place them in the cavity of the bird. Tie the legs together with some kitchen string. Transfer the chicken to a plate, cover with plastic wrap and set aside for 30 minutes.

Put a roasting pan in the preheated oven for 10 minutes to heat up. Pour the remaining olive oil in the roasting pan. Sprinkle sea salt over the chicken, then put the chicken in the tin and roast in the preheated oven for 1 hour.

Remove the chicken from the oven, cover with aluminium foil and let cool for 15 minutes before carving.

Serve slices of the chicken with either Smashed Roast Potatoes or Winter Rosti (see page 147) and freshly shelled peas.

These fantastic little spring leeks are so small they are easily confused with scallions. I have left them pretty much untrimmed in this recipe. The green tips are soft and although they may not be eaten, they do give a more leeky flavor to the dish if left on. With the other ingredients like lemon and soy sauce, you could be forgiven for thinking this is Chinese but the couscous brings it very much into the realms of North Africa. The technique of frying the couscous in a little oil with nuts is not entirely traditional but is foolproof. Just the way I like it. You could also use aromatic spices like paprika and cumin.

lemony chicken with leeks and pine nut couscous

½ cup plain flour

1 organic spring chicken, about 3½ lbs., cut into 10 pieces

½ cup light olive oil

12 baby leeks

3 garlic cloves, chopped

1 unwaxed lemon, thickly sliced

½ cup white wine

½ cup freshly squeezed lemon juice

½ cup chicken stock

1 tablespoon light soy sauce

sea salt and freshly ground black pepper

pine nut couscous:

2 tablespoons light olive oil

2½ tablespoons pine nuts

1⅓ cups couscous

1½ cups chicken stock

Serves 4

Season the flour with sea salt and pepper and put it in a clean plastic bag. Add half the chicken pieces and shake to coat them in the seasoned flour. Repeat with the remaining chicken pieces and set aside until needed.

Heat the olive oil in a large frying pan over a medium/high heat. Add the leeks and stir-fry for 4 minutes, until softened and silky. Remove the leeks from the pan and set aside. Add half of the chicken to the pan and cook in batches for 4–5 minutes, turning each piece often, until golden brown all over. Transfer the browned chicken to a plate and repeat to cook the remaining chicken.

Pour off all but 1 tablespoon of oil from the pan, leaving any sediment in the pan. Add the garlic and lemon and cook for 1 minute, stirring well to combine with any of the cooked on bits on the bottom of the pan. Add the wine and let sizzle for 1 minute, then add the lemon juice, chicken stock, and soy sauce and bring to a boil. Return the chicken to the pan and cook for 20 minutes. Turn each piece of chicken, then put the leeks on top of the chicken. Cover the pan with cooking foil and cook for a further 20 minutes, until the chicken is cooked through. Stir to evenly combine the chicken and any of the cooking juices with the leeks. Cover the pan and set aside while cooking the couscous.

To make the couscous, put the olive oil and pine nuts in a saucepan and cook over high heat, stirring constantly, until the nuts begin to turn golden. Add the couscous and stir for 1 minute, then add the stock which will boil rapidly—quickly stir a couple of times. Turn the heat off, cover with a tight-fitting lid and let stand for 10 minutes. Fluff the couscous with a fork and cover again for 5 minutes. Fluff again to separate as many grains as possible and serve with the lemony chicken.

New season lamb is around in late spring, although it does feel like we can eat lamb all year round. This is due to imports to the northern hemisphere from New Zealand. This reminds us that meat too, and not just fruit and vegetables, follow the natural course of the seasons. Just as pigs are fattened with the windfalls of autumn, baby lambs are fed the nutrient-packed grasses of spring. Try bringing the chops to room temperature before cooking. Unlike chicken, lamb is free from nasty bugs and can be safely left to rest for a short while before cooking. This really does make a difference to the taste and texture of the cooked meat, especially when, as here, you have such a short cooking time. You can prepare the gratin in advance and keep it refrigerated until you are ready to cook it. Use underripe tomatoes as you don't want the cooked gratin to be too sloppy—the greener, the better, especially if you can get your hands on some exotic early season heirloom varieties. The sharpness of underripe tomatoes with the feta is fantastic with the richness of the lamb.

spiced lamb chops with tomato and feta gratin

3 tomatoes, thinly sliced

1 onion, thinly sliced

1 tablespoon fresh oregano

2 oz. marinated or plain feta, crumbled

⅓ cup fresh breadcrumbs

12 lamb chops, trimmed of excess fat

1 teaspoon ground cumin

1 teaspoon ground coriander

light olive oil, for frying

sea salt and freshly ground black pepper

lemon wedges, to serve (optional)

a medium ovenproof dish, lightly buttered

Serves 4

Preheat the oven to 350°F.

Place alternating layers of tomato and onion slices and oregano leaves in the buttered dish. Scatter the feta on top, then sprinkle the breadcrumbs evenly over. Cook in the preheated oven for 40 minutes.

Put the lamb chops on a chopping board and evenly sprinkle each one with the cumin and coriander. Sprinkle some sea salt and grind some black pepper over each chop.

Put a drizzle of the oil in a nonstick frying pan and put over high heat. Cook the lamb in 2 batches for 3 minutes on each side.

Serve the lamb with the tomato and feta gratin and lemon wedges to squeeze over the lamb, if you like.

Traditionally, people included rhubarb in their diets at a time of year when dessert fruit simply wasn't available. Over the last decade its popularity has diminished as imported exotic fruit is so widely available all year round. Happily, there has been a recent resurgence of interest in this wonderfully bizarre vegetable. You will find the delicate, pink "forced" rhubarb in early spring and a few months later the tougher, more astringent outdoor variety arrives. Either will work well in this recipe. Please note, I use the term "cheesecake" loosely here as it has no base.

poached rhubarb with pistachio and orange cheesecake

14 oz. ricotta cheese

½ cup confectioners' sugar

1 egg, lightly beaten

finely grated zest and juice of 1 unwaxed orange

½ cup shelled unsalted pistachios

¼ cup granulated sugar

6 rhubarb stalks, cut into 1½-inch lengths

an 8 x 4-inch loaf pan, lined with parchment paper

Serves 4

Preheat the oven to 350°F.

Put the ricotta in a food processor with the confectioners' sugar, egg, and orange zest and process until smooth. Stir the pistachios in, then spoon the mixture into the lined pan. Press down with the back of a large spoon, cover the tin with aluminium foil, and cook in the preheated oven for 50 minutes. Remove from the oven and let cool before removing from the pan.

Mix the orange juice, sugar, and ½ cup water in a small saucepan. Cook over high heat and boil for 5 minutes. Add the rhubarb and cook for 2–3 minutes over high heat, stirring often, until the rhubarb starts to soften. Transfer to a bowl and let cool to room temperature. Cut the baked ricotta into thick slices and serve with the poached fruit mixture spooned over the top.

Next time: Mix the rhubarb component of this recipe with some lightly whipped cream to make a simple fruit fool. Rhubarb is also lovely in cakes and crumbles. Try substituting the 12 oz. of fresh strawberries in the Strawberry Buttermilk Cake (see page 75) with 2 rhubarb stalks cut into 1-inch pieces. Alternatively, you could serve the ricotta cheesecake with other seasonal fruits—it works a treat with poached or fresh pears in fall or winter.

summer

the tastes of **summer**

The summer months positively hum with a sense of abundance and plenty. The bees are busy, the birds are singing, and mother nature is in full bloom—the countryside thick with plants and wildlife. The fields are verdant and luscious, as are the market gardens which overflow with ripe fruit and vegetables in shades of brilliant green, red, and yellow. Summer is very good news for the organic growers and even better news for us.

Summer is a season that means something different to everyone but it is special everywhere. The days are longer and warmer and it's the season that marks the end of a school year and often the start of family holidays. For me it is the sounds of the ocean, of bare feet running on wooden decks and a chorus of cicadas at dusk. It is a time for reading in the sunshine, taking afternoon swims and enjoying outdoor barbecues with family and friends. And, as the sun chases our blues away, crops such as wheat are turning to gold in the fields and the farmers are already busy preparing stores for the leaner months to come by cutting grass to be stored as hay.

The wondrous **tomato**, the king of the summer crops, is at its peak now. Keep your eyes peeled at the farmers' market for locally grown "heirloom varieties" or why not try growing some yourself from seed? Beefsteak tomatoes are just perfect thickly sliced, seasoned with salt and black pepper and used in a simple salad—their naturally sweet juices combining with a few splashes of fruity extra virgin olive oil to make a light dressing. Sweet little cherry or pomodoro varieties can be tossed with some cubes of leftover stale bread, anchovies, and smoky paprika for a rustic Spanish-style panzanella salad. Try and find baby yellow tomatoes. These can be quickly pan-fried with lemon thyme and served on a bed of indulgent Champagne risotto to make the perfect summer *al fresco* supper. Treat your friends to an upside-down tomato tart seasoned with salty little capers and fresh rosemary then topped with puff pastry and baked until golden. It's delicious, impressive, and simplicity itself to make. **Beans and peas** are at their most sweet and tender throughout the summer months. A

quick blanche in some boiling water is all they need to ready them for use in a multitude of summer dishes. Try putting any waxy beans with walnuts, bacon, and Gorgonzola to make a satisfying salad, or cook an effortless pasta sauce using sugary-sweet young peas, crème fraîche, and refreshingly zingy mint.

Eggplants are heavy and ripe now too, their skins a gloriously shiny deep purple. They go so well with just about any flavor or cooking style you choose. Spice them up with Middle Eastern flavourings and enjoy them with a speedy couscous. Cook thick chunks of eggplant in a rich, fruity tomato and basil sauce and bake it with some fresh pasta. **Baby zucchini** are a perfect pairing with pasta too—try them fried until crisp with garlic and chile and tossed through spaghetti. **Corn-on-the-cob** is squeakily fresh, its creamy kernels perfect for adding to a clear Chinese-style sweetcorn and chicken soup or used as the base for a salsa to enjoy with sticky ribs, ideal for entertaining at a barbecue.

Enjoy the availability of fresh **fish and seafood**. Try a light summer stew of shellfish, tomato, and couscous, a piece of crispy-skinned salmon with a tangy salsa verde rice (seasoned with a mixture of fresh **green herbs**) or a fragrant Thai-style eggplant and fish curry.

Summer is the time when soft fruit becomes downright sexy. Early season cherries, bursting with sweetness and flavor are crying out to be used in a clafoutis, surely the simplest and most delicious of all baked desserts. Berries are available in abundance. They are always delicious on their own but for something different why not try baking a rich strawberry buttermilk cake or a blackberry crumble? Stone fruits also come into their own now. Use fresh **plums** to make a delicious sauce to serve with crispy-skinned duck. Choose **peaches** from your local farmers' market that are soft-fleshed and fragrant. You'll find that locally-grown organic varieties are smaller than their trucked-in counterparts but have a flavor that will knock your socks off. Try serving juicy slices of peach with a frisée salad and some melt-in-the-mouth fresh mozzarella.

spanish-style panzanella

When summer is in full swing there is no excuse for not using fantastic tomatoes. They should be full and firm, fire-engine red, and the leafy top should smell like freshly cut grass. This classic Tuscan salad is given a decidedly Spanish edge with a few Iberian specialities thrown in, such as the white anchovies and the smoky paprika known as "pimentón de la Vera." This is a gorgeous spice and is usually sold in very decorative tins, my favorite being the one with a small image of a bride and groom on the side. It is also one of the hidden spices in chorizo sausage.

1 yellow bell pepper
6 ripe tomatoes, chopped
1 Spanish onion, thinly sliced into rings
1 large handful of flatleaf parsley leaves, roughly chopped
8 white marinated anchovies, thinly sliced
4 slices of sourdough bread, crusts removed
¼ cup extra virgin olive oil
2 tablespoons sherry vinegar
½ teaspoon Spanish paprika
1 garlic clove, crushed
3½ oz. Manchego cheese, shaved (optional)

a ridged stovetop grill pan

Serves 4

Preheat the grill pan over high heat. Cook the bell pepper in the pan until the skin is blackened and puffed all over. Place in a clean plastic bag. When cool enough to handle, peel the pepper, discard the seeds and membrane and slice the flesh. Put in a bowl with the tomatoes, onion, parsley, and anchovies.

Grill or toast the bread until golden. Tear each slice into 4–5 pieces and add to the bowl with the other ingredients.

Mix the olive oil, vinegar, paprika, and garlic in a bowl and pour over the salad, tossing everything to combine. Leave for 10 minutes before gently tossing through the cheese shavings, if using, to serve.

mozzarella, peach, and frisée salad

I am a big fan of fresh mozzarella, as used in this recipe. Made from cow's or buffalo's milk, these soft white balls of cheese are best enjoyed within a day or two of being made. The cheese is quite different from the firmer, yellow variety you may be familiar with which is often used on pizza and lasagne. All sorts of tricks are performed on peaches to keep them from ripening when they have to travel long distances so it's really worth getting your hands on some fuzzy and fragrant locally grown ones.

3 fresh peaches, cut into thin wedges
4 handfuls of frisée leaves, trimmed
1 large ball of fresh mozzarella, torn into thin shreds
3 tablespoons extra virgin olive oil
1 tablespoon white wine vinegar
freshly ground black pepper

Serves 4, as a starter

Put the peach wedges and frisée in a large bowl and gently toss to mix. Arrange on a serving plate. Scatter the mozzarella pieces over the salad.

Put the olive oil, vinegar and black pepper in a bowl, whisk with a fork, and then spoon over the salad to serve.

Next time: Replace the mozzarella with 5 oz. crumbled firm blue cheese and the frisée with spinach leaves. Or, alternatively, keep the mozzarella and replace the other ingredients with fresh slices of tomato, basil leaves, and some fruity extra virgin olive oil for a traditionally Italian *Insalata Caprese*.

See photograph on page 48.

figs with crispy prosciutto, blue cheese, and arugula

The flavors in this salad are so simple and classic so here's the trick—get your hands on the best produce and all the hard work is done already! Have the prosciutto sliced fresh from the leg at the deli and you will notice the difference. You don't have to cook the prosciutto to a crisp if you prefer not to, but I do think the crispy texture goes so well with sweet honey-flavored figs, in the same way crispy bacon works with maple syrup. In a frost-free area you may find fresh figs in the very early days of summer.

3 tablespoons light olive oil
6 thin slices of prosciutto
2 tablespoons red wine vinegar
1 teaspoon Dijon mustard
3–4 oz. arugula
6 figs, quartered
5 oz. firm blue cheese (such as Roquefort or Maytag Blue), crumbled
sea salt and freshly ground black pepper

Serves 4, as a starter

Heat the olive oil in a nonstick frying pan over medium heat and cook the prosciutto for 1 minute on each side, until crispy, and place on paper towels. When cool enough to handle, break the prosciutto into smaller pieces. Pour the oil from the pan into a small bowl and add the vinegar, mustard, a pinch of sea salt, and freshly ground black pepper to taste.

Arrange the arugula on a serving plate with the fig quarters on top. Scatter over the cheese and the proscuitto pieces and pour the dressing evenly over the salad to serve.

See photograph on page 49.

wax beans with walnuts, bacon, and Gorgonzola

Hand pick your beans for this recipe. Basically you can use whichever one you fancy, but in early summer the young green beans or a stringless variety of runner bean will be sweeter and crunchier than larger, older green beans. True, yellow wax beans may not be as tasty but their color, texture, and crunch factor is good enough to include them in any salad, especially one that combines the perfect flavor combination of smoky, crispy bits of bacon with a strong-flavored blue cheese such as Gorgonzola.

3½ oz. green beans, ends trimmed
3½ oz. yellow wax beans, ends trimmed
2 tablespoons light olive oil
2 slices of bacon, thinly sliced
⅓ cup walnut halves
2 tablespoons red wine vinegar
3½ oz. Gorgonzola cheese, crumbled
freshly ground black pepper

Serves 4, as a starter

Bring a saucepan of water to the boil, add the beans and cook for 2 minutes. Drain and run under cold water until completely cool. Drain well and put in a bowl.

Put the olive oil in a nonstick frying pan over medium heat and add the bacon slices. Cook for 3–4 minutes, stirring often so the bacon turns an even, golden brown. Add the walnuts and cook for a further 2–3 minutes.

Remove from the heat and add the vinegar and some black pepper. Add the beans to the pan, toss to coat in the bacon mixture, then add the Gorgonzola. Toss to combine and allow the cheese to soften before arranging the salad on a serving platter.

There is a good reason why Chinese cuisine has been so influential and remains popular. When done well it pays the utmost respect to fresh ingredients, cooking them quickly and with a minimum of fuss. Fresh corn, bursting with flavor and sweetness, is the main player here, subtly enhanced with fresh ginger. Ginger has an almost celestial status in Chinese cooking and, when used with scallions, brings balance and harmony to other ingredients.

fresh corn and chicken soup

1 organic chicken breast fillet (about 8 oz.) cut into 1-inch cubes

1 tablespoon cornstarch

1 tablespoon light soy sauce

1 tablespoon Chinese rice wine (or dry sherry)

1 tablespoon vegetable oil

2 teaspoons finely grated fresh ginger

2 scallions, thinly sliced

1 leek, thinly sliced

1 celery rib, thinly sliced

2 ears of fresh corn, husked, kernels cut from cobs with serrated knife

2 quarts chicken stock

½ teaspoon sea salt

½ teaspoon sugar

½ teaspoon white pepper

1 large handful of cilantro, leaves and stems, roughly chopped

Serves 4

Put the chicken, cornstarch, soy sauce, and rice wine in a bowl and stir well. Cover and refrigerate for 1 hour.

Heat the oil in a saucepan over high heat and cook the ginger, scallions, leek, and celery for 2–3 minutes, until softened but not brown.

Add the corn kernels and cook for 1 minute. Add the stock and the sea salt, sugar, and white pepper and bring to a boil. Reduce the heat to a low simmer and cook for 10 minutes.

Add the chicken and marinade to the soup, stirring to separate the chicken pieces, cover and cook for 5 minutes, until the chicken is cooked.

Divide the cilantro among 4 serving bowls and ladle the soup over to serve.

Next time: This light soup can be made more substantial and hearty with the addition of lightly beaten egg. Whisk 2 organic eggs in a bowl until just combined and slowly pour them into the simmering soup in a steady stream. Using a chopstick, gently stir for an authentic-looking Chinese soup. Ladle into serving bowls and drizzle some sesame oil over the top to serve.

Ricotta is an Italian cheese made from the whey that is the by-product of making mozzarella and provolone. I think it is the most versatile of cheeses as it can be used in a wide variety of dishes, both sweet and savory, including salads, pasta dishes, and pancakes. Here ricotta is baked and can be made the day before if you like. Served warm or cold, this is almost too easy and too good!

baked ricotta with roasted cherry tomato salsa

1 lb. ricotta cheese

½ teaspoon sea salt

1 egg

¼ cup grated Parmesan cheese

¼ cup olive oil

2 garlic cloves, sliced

12 cherry tomatoes, cut in half

1 tablespoon sherry vinegar

½ teaspoon caster sugar

10–12 fresh basil leaves, finely sliced

½ red onion, finely diced

sea salt and freshly ground black pepper

toasted sourdough bread, to serve (optional)

a 5 x 5 x 3-inch deep cake pan, lined with baking parchment

Serves 4

Preheat the oven to 350°F.

Put the ricotta in a bowl with ½ teaspoon sea salt, the egg, and Parmesan and stir well. Spoon into the lined pan and bake in the preheated oven for 50 minutes. Remove from the oven and let cool before inverting onto a chopping board.

Put the olive oil in a frying pan over high heat and cook the garlic and tomatoes for 2 minutes, shaking the pan, so the tomatoes cook evenly and start to split and soften.

Remove from the heat, stir in the vinegar, sugar, basil, and onion and season to taste with sea salt and black pepper.

Cut the ricotta into 4 thick slices and serve with the salsa spooned over the top and the toasted sourdough on the side, if using.

Next time: Preheat the oven to 350°F. Divide the ricotta mixture into 4 and roll each portion up in fresh sheets of lasagne to make cannelloni logs. Place the cannelloni side by side in a small baking dish, pour over 1 cup fresh tomato sauce and top with some slices of firm mozzarella. Bake in the preheated oven until golden and bubbling hot.

Popping its head up in just about every style of cuisine, the summer-fruiting eggplant is very versatile. It is just as much at home steamed with scallions and fresh ginger as it is with tomato, basil and pecorino or, as in this dish, with Moroccan spices. You will need one large eggplant, so look for a beauty that is firm, full, and heavy with shiny deep-purple skin. The couscous recipe alone is a treat and can be made on its own for any other occasion.

spiced eggplant
couscous

¼ cup vegetable oil

1 large eggplant, cut into 1-inch cubes

1 tablespoon light olive oil

1⅓ cups couscous

½ teaspoon paprika

½ teaspoon ground red chile

1½ cups chicken stock

1 small bunch of cilantro, leaves and stems, roughly chopped

2 oz. baby spinach

½ cup plain yogurt

lemon wedges, to serve

Serves 4

Heat the vegetable oil in frying pan over high heat and cook the eggplant for 3–4 minutes, turning often so it is an even, golden brown all over. Place on paper towels to drain off the excess oil.

Heat the olive oil in a saucepan over medium heat. Add the couscous, paprika, and ground chile pepper and cook for 2 minutes, stirring constantly. Add the stock and bring to a boil. Remove the pan from the heat, cover with a tight-fitting lid and let stand for 10 minutes.

Fluff the couscous with a fork, then cover and leave for a further 5 minutes. Place the couscous in a large bowl and add the eggplant, cilantro, and baby spinach and toss to combine.

Place on a serving plate with the yogurt and lemon wedges on the side to serve.

Next time: Replace the eggplant with 3 summer ripe zucchini, cut into ½-inch wide rounds. Pan-fry them in a little light olive oil until golden on both sides. Add the zucchini to the prepared couscous with a handful of roughly chopped fresh mint.

spaghettini with baby peas and mint

Be sure to use fresh baby peas for this simple pasta dish. Just like a ripe tomato, young peas contain higher levels of glutamate than the larger more mature pea. Glutamate is one of the natural occurring chemicals which enhance the flavors in fresh food—this is why young peas and ripe tomatoes taste so good.

16 oz. spaghettini, or similar pasta
½ cup freshly shelled peas
½ cup crème fraîche or sour cream
1 handful of fresh mint leaves, finely chopped
sea salt and freshly ground black pepper

Serves 4, as a starter

Cook the pasta according to the packet instructions. About 2 minutes before the pasta is cooked add the peas to the boiling water.

Drain well and return the pasta and peas to the warm pan with the crème fraîche and mint. Gently toss to combine and to coat the pasta in the softened crème fraîche. Season well with sea salt and black pepper and serve immediately.

Next time: For a simple variation using Italian bacon, chop 4 thin slices of pancetta and cook in 2 tablespoons sizzling butter until lightly colored. Add 2 finely chopped tomatoes, ½ cup fresh peas and ½ cup light cream to the pan and cook over medium heat for a few minutes, until the sauce has thickened a little and the peas are cooked. Stir in ½ cup finely grated Parmesan cheese and season with sea salt and black pepper. Add the sauce to the cooked pasta, stir well, and serve with extra grated Parmesan sprinkled over the top.

spaghetti with chile zucchini crumbs

This is one of those pasta combinations that works with just about any of your favorite seasonings. You can easily use red pepper flakes instead of fresh chiles or throw in a few chopped anchovies if you are a fan. Even if you aren't, anchovies will cook down and dissipate into the sauce and you won't even know they are there. When it comes to the flavor of zucchini, size does matter. Like most green vegetables, the younger, the tastier so use small ones here, no longer than 6 inches for a really simple yet delicious pasta sauce. And do use good bread, even if it is stale. The flavor of a loaf intensifies as it becomes stale. A cheap white loaf will always make really nasty, cheap, white crumbs.

14 oz. spaghetti, or similar pasta
6 tablespoons light olive oil
¾ cup fresh breadcrumbs
8 small or baby zucchini, cut into julienne strips
2 garlic cloves, grated
2 small red chiles, deseeded and chopped
finely grated Parmesan cheese, to serve

Serves 4

Cook the spaghetti according to the packet instructions. Drain well and return to the pan to keep warm.

Meanwhile, heat a large frying pan over medium heat. When it is hot, add half of the oil, swirling around to coat the pan, then add the breadcrumbs. Cook the crumbs for 3–4 minutes, stirring constantly until evenly browned with a nutty aroma. Remove from the pan and wipe the pan clean.

Add the remaining oil to the pan and cook the zucchini for 5 minutes over high heat, turning often, until golden and starting to look crispy. Add the garlic and chiles and cook for 4–5 minutes, stirring often.

Add the cooked pasta and breadcrumbs to the pan, tossing around to combine and serve immediately with grated Parmesan sprinkled over the top.

baked ziti with eggplant, basil, and ricotta

14 oz. ziti, or other large tube shaped pasta, such as rigatoni

¾ cup light olive oil

1 eggplant, halved and cut into very thin slices

1 onion, chopped

2 garlic cloves, chopped

3 tomatoes, chopped

1 small handful of basil leaves, torn

½ cup red wine

4 oz. ricotta cheese

½ cup grated pecorino cheese

sea salt and freshly ground black pepper

a large ovenproof baking dish

Serves 4

Do not refrigerate tomatoes! Tomatoes picked before they are fully mature will keep on ripening and they do so correctly at room temperature. This sauce should be sweet and fruity so it's the perfect dish to make use of tomatoes that have been sitting in your fruit bowl, turning all lovely, soft and over ripe. It's important to use a light olive oil here; extra virgin olive oil burns at a lower temperature and will make the eggplant bitter and oily.

Preheat the oven to 425°F. Cook the pasta according to the packet instructions. Drain well and return to the warm pan.

Heat the olive oil in a frying pan and when it is hot, but not smoking, cook the eggplant slices, in batches, for 2 minutes on each side, until golden. Remove and place on paper towels. Repeat to cook all of the eggplant. Pour off all but 1 tablespoon of oil from the frying pan, add the onion and garlic and cook for 2–3 minutes, stirring often. Add the tomatoes, basil, and red wine, 1 cup water, sea salt, and black pepper to taste and bring to a boil. Boil for 10 minutes, until you have a thickened sauce. Stir in the eggplant then add to the pasta and stir well.

Put the mixture in a large baking dish. Spoon the ricotta on top, sprinkle over the pecorino and bake in the preheated oven for 20 minutes until golden and crispy around the edges.

It seems reasonable for me to suggest that we tend to drink more Champagne and sparkling wine in summer. If there is a rare occasion where you have a glass or so left over, why not use it in this light and summery risotto? Or, conversely, open a bottle just to use what you need for this recipe and drink the remainder while you are stirring the risotto! You could cook off the tomatoes beforehand and reheat them once the risotto is ready. It's all too easy and makes a perfect, light summer supper.

Champagne risotto with lemon thyme tomatoes

1 quart vegetable or chicken stock

1 cup Champagne or other sparkling white wine, such as cava or prosecco

3 tablespoons butter

1 leek, thinly sliced

1 garlic clove, finely chopped

1½ cups Arborio rice

½ cup finely grated Parmesan cheese

1 tablespoon light olive oil

16–20 small yellow tomatoes

2 sprigs fresh lemon thyme

Parmesan shavings, to serve

sea salt and freshly ground black pepper

Serves 4

Put the stock and Champagne in a saucepan over medium heat and gently simmer.

Put 2 tablespoons of the butter in a heavy-based saucepan over medium heat. When the butter is sizzling, add the leek and garlic to the pan and cook for 4–5 minutes, until the leek has softened but not browned.

Add the rice and cook for 1 minute, stirring well. Add a small ladle of the hot stock mixture to the pan and stir for a few minutes, until almost all the stock has been absorbed. Repeat until all the stock has been added and the rice is soft but still firm to the bite, adding a little extra water if necessary. Stir in the remaining butter and the Parmesan and cover the pan until needed.

Put the olive oil in a frying pan over medium heat. Add the tomatoes, lemon thyme sprigs, sea salt, and black pepper to the pan and cook for 3–4 minutes, shaking the pan, until the tomatoes have softened and are just starting to split.

Serve the risotto in bowls with the lemon thyme tomatoes on top and offer Parmesan shavings on the side for sprinkling.

What exactly is an heirloom tomato? Schools of thought vary and include a system of classification based on age (that is, the age of the seed) or my favorite which is thinking of the heirloom as a tomato variety that has been nurtured, handed down from generation to generation, or kept within a family. Whatever the case, you will find a story behind each heirloom variety but be sure to choose one that stays relatively firm when cooked. I have used fresh rosemary and little capers here to flavor what is essentially a tomato *tarte tatin*, but you could add any combination of ingredients that takes your fancy, such as Ligurian olives, oregano, garlic, or anchovies.

upside-down heirloom tomato tart

2 tablespoons light olive oil

2 teaspoons small capers, rinsed if salted

10–12 fresh rosemary needles

3 ripe tomatoes, thickly sliced

12 oz.-sheet ready-rolled puff pastry dough, defrosted if frozen

cracked black pepper

extra virgin olive oil, for drizzling

a nonstick, heatproof frying pan 8–9 inches across

Serves 4, as a starter

Preheat the oven to 425°F.

Put the oil, capers, and rosemary in a heatproof nonstick frying pan. Put over high heat and when the capers start to sizzle add the tomatoes, firmly pressing them down in a single layer in the pan. Cook for 3–4 minutes to allow the tomatoes to sizzle and soften.

Place the sheet of pastry over the tomatoes, folding in the corners, being careful not to press down on the tomatoes. Transfer the pan to the preheated oven and cook for 18–20 minutes, until the pastry is puffed and golden. Remove the pan from the oven and let the tart rest for a couple of minutes.

Place a serving plate that is larger than the frying pan upside-down on top of the pan and quickly flip the pan over so the tart falls onto the plate. Sprinkle with cracked black pepper and a drizzle of olive oil and cut into 4 wedges to serve.

Next time: Make a roasted tomato sauce using prime summer tomatoes. Cut 6 medium tomatoes in half and place them on a baking sheet, cut side up, with 1 sliced red onion, 3 sliced garlic cloves, 2 tablespoons olive oil and ½ teaspoon each of sea salt and sugar sprinkled over. Bake in a preheated oven at 325°F for 1½ hours. Remove from the oven and process in a food processor with 3–4 fresh basil leaves, until you have a chunky sauce. Serve tossed with the pasta of your choice.

This is a very simple and tasty summer dish featuring ripe tomatoes with a combination of really fresh seafood. Once you become more familiar with the recipe you can add any combination of your favorite seafood—pieces of salmon fillet (replacing the white fish) would work very well. Couscous shows its versatility in this recipe too, acting as a thickener, like rice, pasta, or barley, and turning a soup into a light stew.

shellfish, tomato, and couscous stew

2 tablespoons light olive oil

12 large uncooked shrimp, shelled and deveined

4 small squid, hoods cut into ½-inch wide pieces

1 red onion, chopped

1 garlic clove, chopped

1 small red bell pepper, thinly sliced

3 cups chicken stock

2 tomatoes, chopped

3 heaped tablespoons couscous

10–12 saffron threads

10 oz. any white fish fillet, cut into bite-sized cubes

12 mussels, scrubbed and cleaned of beards

1 large handful of fresh parsley, roughly chopped

sea salt and freshly ground black pepper

lemon wedges, to serve (optional)

Serves 4

Heat the olive oil in a saucepan over high heat and cook the prawns for 1 minute on each side. Remove and place in a large bowl. Add the squid to the pan and cook for 1 minute. Remove and put in the bowl with the prawns. Add the onion, garlic, and bell pepper to the pan and cook for 4–5 minutes, stirring often.

Add the stock, tomatoes, couscous, and saffron to the pan and bring to a boil. Taste for seasoning and add sea salt and black pepper as required. Reduce the heat and simmer for 5 minutes. Add the white fish and mussels to the pan, cover and cook for 10 minutes, until the fish is cooked and the mussels have opened. (Discard any mussels that haven't opened.) Stir in the squid and shrimp and cook for 2 minutes.

Serve in bowls with the parsley scattered over the top and the lemon wedges on the side to squeeze over, if using.

fragrant eggplant and fish curry

Little pea and apple eggplants are often used in traditional Thai curries. They are aptly named but they are also quite bitter and difficult to find. Even though I have local markets which supply them, I still prefer to use the larger, more conventional eggplant. Its flesh is not so bitter and it is unctuous, almost velvet soft, when cooked. The technique given here for boiling the coconut cream for several minutes prior to adding the curry paste is called "cracking the cream." This method separates the oils from the liquid in the cream and then allows the curry paste to be fried without using extra oil. It will also give you a curry which will look and taste like the real deal.

2 tablespoons Thai green curry paste
1 teaspoon green peppercorns in brine
2 tablespoons vegetable oil
2 eggplants, cut into ½-inch slices
1 cup coconut cream
2 cups coconut milk
1 tablespoon Thai fish sauce
2 teaspoons sugar
1 lb. any white fish fillet, cut into bite-sized cubes
5 oz. baby corn, cut in half lengthways
4–6 kaffir lime leaves, torn
2 handfuls of Thai basil or basil leaves
1 large red chile, thinly sliced
boiled jasmine rice, to serve

Serves 4

Pound the curry paste with the peppercorns in a pestle and mortar.

Heat the oil in a saucepan and cook the eggplant over high heat for 2 minutes on each side. Remove the eggplant and drain on paper towels. (You may need to do this in batches.)

Put the coconut cream in the saucepan over high heat and boil for 3–4 minutes. Stir in the curry paste mixture. Let the mixture simmer for 5 minutes, stirring often. It will look like it has broken. Stir in the sugar and fish sauce and cook for a further 2 minutes.

Add the coconut milk, bring to a boil, then add the white fish pieces, corn, eggplant, and lime leaves. Reduce the heat and simmer for 10 minutes, until the fish is cooked through. Stir in half of the basil and sprinkle the remaining basil leaves and chile over the top. Serve with boiled jasmine rice.

crispy-skinned salmon with salsa verde rice

I am a big fan of a good rice salad and it's the salsa verde that is the star here. You could make the rice salad ahead of time for a barbecue and simply cook the well-seasoned fish on a searing hot grill. The literal translation of salsa verde is "green sauce." The classic Italian salsa verde uses parsley as its base but I have extended it here to use just about as many fresh green summer herbs as I could find, including fresh celery leaves. You might call it a salsa *molto* verde—a *very* green sauce!

1½ cups medium grain brown rice
2 tablespoons vegetable oil
4 salmon fillets, 6 oz. each, skin on
sea salt and freshly ground black pepper
lemon wedges, to serve

salsa verde:
1 large handful of fresh parsley, chopped
1 large handful of fresh basil leaves
1 large handful of celery leaves
6 scallions, thinly sliced
4 anchovy fillets in oil
2 tablespoons capers
½ cup extra virgin olive oil
¼ cup freshly squeezed lemon juice

Serves 4

To make the salsa verde, put the herbs, celery, and scallions in a food processor and process until roughly combined. Add the anchovies, 1 teaspoon of the oil from the anchovy jar, and the capers and process for a few seconds. With the machine running, add the olive oil in a steady stream until it is all incorporated. Transfer the mixture to a bowl, stir in the lemon juice and season well with sea salt and black pepper. Cover and set aside until needed. Cook the rice in boiling water. It should be just cooked but still a bit firm to the bite. Rinse under cold water and drain very well. Transfer to a bowl and stir in the salsa verde.

Season the skin of the salmon well with sea salt and black pepper. Heat the vegetable oil in a heavy-based frying pan over high heat. When the oil is very hot, add the fish, skin side-down and cook for 2 minutes until the skin is golden and crispy. Turn the salmon over and cook for a further 2 minutes. Serve the fish with the salsa verde rice and lemon wedges on the side to squeeze over.

See photograph on page 70.

crispy-skinned duck with fresh plum sauce

Plum sauce with duck is not a new idea but it is a good one. Unfortunately something bad happened along the way and now we are often confronted with ready-made plum sauces which are so sickly sweet they could be served on ice cream! Making your own is easy and this recipe achieves the perfect balance of sweet, salty and sour.

4 duck breasts, 8 oz. each, skin on
2 teaspoons Chinese five-spice powder
1 teaspoon ground white pepper
1 teaspoon sea salt
½ cup vegetable oil
boiled white rice, to serve (optional)

plum sauce:
¾ cup plus 2 tablespoons granulated sugar
8 plums, halved and pitted
1 cinnamon stick
2 star anise
1 tablespoon Thai fish sauce
1 tablespoon white wine vinegar

a bamboo steamer, lined with rice paper

Serves 4

To make the plum sauce, put the sugar and ¾ cup water in a small saucepan and bring to a boil, stirring until the sugar dissolves and the mixture looks syrupy. Add the plums, cinnamon, and star anise and simmer for 2–3 minutes. Remove from the heat and stir in the fish sauce and vinegar. Put the sauce in a bowl, cover and set aside to let the flavors develop.

Rub the duck breast skin with the five-spice powder, pepper, and salt. Use toothpicks to pin the end pieces of skin to the meat to prevent it from retracting when cooked. Put the duck in a bamboo steamer, cover with a lid, and place over a saucepan of boiling water for 20–25 minutes. Put the duck on a plate and refrigerate.

Heat the vegetable oil in a nonstick frying pan over medium/high heat. Add the duck, skin side-down, and cook for 3 minutes, until the skin is crisp and dark brown. Turn the duck over and cook for a further 2 minutes. Put the duck on a chopping board, cover with aluminium foil, and let rest for 5 minutes. Cut each duck breast into thick slices, spoon over the plum sauce and serve with rice.

See photograph on page 71.

sticky spareribs with fresh corn salsa

These lip-smackingly good ribs are basted and then left in a full-flavored marinade overnight. It is so important to use fresh sweetcorn for the salsa and shuck it just before cooking. The best way to keep vegetables fresh is to store them in their natural skins so don't buy cobs smothered with plastic. Instead, look for summer-ripened ones still in their silky skins.

1 cup pure maple syrup
½ cup packed brown sugar
1½ cups cider vinegar
½ cup Thai fish sauce
2 garlic cloves
10–12 large dried red chiles (Kashmiri)
8 long spareribs, ideally 4–6 inches

corn salsa:
3 tablespoons light olive oil
1½ cups fresh corn kernels (from 2 ears)
1 small red onion, chopped
1 large red chile, deseeded and finely chopped
2 tablespoons red wine vinegar
1 small bunch of fresh cilantro, chopped
1 large handful of fresh mint leaves, chopped

Serves 4

Put the maple syrup, sugar, vinegar, fish sauce, garlic, and chiles in a saucepan and bring to a boil, stirring constantly, until the sugar has dissolved. Simmer for 10 minutes until the mixture has thickened. Remove from the heat and let cool. Put the ribs in a large flat dish with the marinade, cover, and refrigerate overnight, turning the ribs often in the marinade.

To make the salsa, heat 1 tablespoon of the olive oil in a frying pan over high heat. Add the corn and cook for 4–5 minutes, stirring often, until the kernels start to turn golden. Add the onion and chile and stir for 1 minute to just soften the onions a little. Remove from the heat and let cool. Stir in the remaining olive oil, vinegar, cilantro, and mint.

Put the ribs and marinade in a single layer on a baking sheet and cook in a preheated oven at 400°F for 30 minutes. Turn the ribs and return them to the oven for a further 10–15 minutes. (If the ribs start to stick to the tray in the final few minutes of cooking, reduce the temperature to 350°F.) Serve with the salsa and any remaining marinade spooned over.

strawberry buttermilk cake

Sweet summer strawberries are so good you will want to eat a whole bowl on their own. I am not a huge fan of the cooked strawberry but occasionally you will come across a great recipe, like this one—a smooth, dense cake given a light and creamy crumb by using buttermilk. It can be made in a conventional round cake tin or baked in a rectanglular tin and cut into squares to serve. The size of a strawberry doesn't determine the sweetness or taste. Little ones are fine left whole but do cut large ones in half before folding them through the batter.

2 cups self-rising flour
1 cup plus 2 tablespoons granulated sugar
1 stick unsalted butter, softened
2 eggs
1 cup buttermilk
12 oz. strawberries, hulled, large ones halved
heavy cream, to serve

crumble topping:
5 tablespoons all-purpose flour
½ a stick unsalted butter, chilled and cubed
½ cup packed brown sugar

an 8-inch square baking pan, greased and lined

Serves 6–8

Preheat the oven to 350°F. Put the flour and sugar in a bowl and mix. Put the butter, eggs, and buttermilk in a food processor and process until smooth and combined. With the motor running, add the flour and sugar and process until well mixed. Scrape down the sides of the bowl to evenly incorporate all the ingredients. Transfer the mixture to a bowl and stir in the strawberries. Spoon the batter into the lined baking pan.

To make the crumble topping, put the flour and butter in a bowl and, using the tips of your fingers, rub the butter into the flour until the mixture resembles coarse breadcrumbs. Stir in the sugar.

Evenly sprinkle the topping mixture over the cake and bake in the preheated oven for 50 minutes, until golden brown on top.

Let cool before cutting into slices or squares and serving with a dollop of heavy cream.

peach and raspberry scone cake

Somewhere between an American shortcake and a scone, this cake has all the hallmarks of a great recipe—it's easy, delicious and has the "I can't believe I made this myself" factor. Because the method is so simple the final result is largely dependent on the quality of the fruit used, so do choose the best peaches, still firm with that heady peach fragrance. I have combined fresh peaches with summer raspberries because they seem to naturally belong together—both in look and in taste. But do feel free to experiment. Try spreading the cake with blackberry jam and topping with plump summer blackberries for an uncompromising alternative.

2¾ cups self-rising flour
2 cups whipping cream
1 cup lemonade
½ cup raspberry jam
2 peaches, pitted and sliced
1 basket fresh raspberries

an 8-inch, loose-bottomed tart tin, lightly greased

Serves 8

Preheat the oven to 350°F. Put the flour in a large bowl and make a well in the centre. Add half of the cream and all the lemonade and use a wooden spoon to mix together.

Spoon the mixture into the prepared tin, gently pressing down to fit, and bake in the preheated oven for 30–35 minutes, until golden brown on top. Remove the cake from the oven and let cool.

Using a long, sharp knife, slice about ¼ inch off the top of the cake to create an even surface. Spread the jam evenly over the top of the cake.

Whip the remaining cream until soft peaks form. Spoon the cream on top of the cake, arrange the fruit on top and cut into wedges to serve.

See photograph on page 76.

melon ice cream

Fruit-flavored ice creams or *gelati* are very popular all over southern Italy but especially loved in Sicily where you will find all sorts of summer market fruits are used. When shopping for a melon, use your nose. It should be musky and fresh without any bruises on the skin. This ice cream can be served with a fresh summer fruit salad or scooped and sandwiched in a little brioche.

1 large cantaloupe, peeled, deseeded, and cut into chunks
½ cup plus 2 tablespoons granulated sugar
2 tablespoons freshly squeezed lemon juice
1¼ cups heavy cream
fresh raspberries, to serve (optional)

an ice cream maker (optional)

Serves 4

Put the melon chunks, sugar, and lemon juice in a food processor and process until chunky. Let the mixture rest in the processor for 30 minutes, then process again until smooth.

Put the cream in a small saucepan and heat over medium heat, stirring often. Don't bring it to a boil.

When the cream is bubbling around the sides of the pan, pour it into the food processor, with the motor running, until well mixed with the melon mixture. Transfer to a bowl and let cool. Put the mixture into an ice cream maker, if using, and churn until firm. Spoon into a container and freeze overnight.

Alternatively, put the mixture in a freezerproof container and freeze for 3 hours, or until the mixture begins to set around the edges. Beat well. Repeat this process every 2 hours until the mixture is firm, then freeze overnight before serving.

Serve balls of the melon ice cream with fresh raspberries.

See photograph on page 77.

cherry and almond clafoutis

Who said summer cooking couldn't include comfort food? Traditionally, the fruit baked in this very classic French dessert were the first cherries of the season, although this recipe would make an equally lovely pudding using other stone fruits such as small peaches, nectarines, or apricots. But what I love most about the clafoutis is that it can all be prepared the day before, the batter kept in the refrigerator overnight and simply poured over the fruit and baked when you are ready for dessert.

1 cup blanched almonds
1 vanilla bean (optional)
3 tablespoons all-purpose flour
1¼ cups granulated sugar
4 eggs
2 egg yolks
1 cup light cream
8 oz. cherries, torn in half and pitted

a round ovenproof dish 8–9 inches across

Serves 4

Preheat the oven to 425°F.

Put the almonds on a baking sheet and toast them in the preheated oven for 6–8 minutes, until lightly golden. Remove and let cool. Put the cooled almonds in a food processor and process until they resemble a coarse meal. Scrape the seeds from the vanilla bean into the food processor with the almonds and process until the mixture resembles a coarse meal. Add the flour and sugar and process to mix. Add the eggs, egg yolks, and cream and process again until you have a smooth, thick batter. Transfer to a bowl, cover and refrigerate until needed. This mixture will keep for 2 days in the refrigerator.

Put the torn cherry halves in the bottom on an ovenproof dish. Carefully pour the batter over the cherries. If need be, rearrange the cherries to evenly distribute. (If using refrigerated batter, beat it until well mixed before pouring over the cherries.)

Cook in the preheated oven for 25 minutes, until the clafoutis is puffed up and golden brown. Allow to cool for a few minutes before serving. The clafoutis will sink during this time.

Serve the clafoutis hot with vanilla ice cream.

blackberry crumble

12 oz. blackberries (about 2 baskets)

1 tablespoon granulated sugar

1 teaspoon cornstarch

1 cup all-purpose flour

5 tablespoons unsalted butter, cubed and chilled

¼ cup packed light brown sugar

heavy cream, to serve

a medium ovenproof dish, lightly buttered

Serves 4

Fresh berries are so tasty and good just as they are that it's tempting not to fuss with them too much. That said, they are also very good used in a crumble—the tastiest of baked desserts. The floral aroma of blackberries can be enhanced by adding a small splash of Middle Eastern rosewater or orange blossom extract to the berries. Keep this in mind whenever you are serving or cooking with blackberries or any red berry.

Preheat the oven to 350°F.

Put the blackberries in a bowl with the granulated sugar and the cornstarch and toss to mix. Tumble the berries into the buttered baking dish and set aside for 15–20 minutes.

Put the flour and butter in a large bowl and, using the tips of your fingers, rub the butter into the flour until the mixture resembles coarse breadcrumbs. Stir in the brown sugar.

Sprinkle the mixture evenly over the berries and bake in the preheated oven for 45–50 minutes, until the top is golden brown.

Let the crumble cool slightly before serving with dollops of cream spooned on top.

fall

the tastes of fall

Fall weather can be very fickle but this is what I love most about the season. I believe fall food should be treated like clothing. Just as one day the temperature suggests a T-shirt but the next it demands a warm scarf, you will need a selection of versatile recipes to see you through a variety of weather conditions and moods. Thankfully, it's also the time of year when we have plenty of choice, as a lot of seasonal foods are in their prime, providing us with a cornucopia of good things to eat.

There is a crossover period between the fruit and vegetables of late summer and the new season's crop that is just beginning to arrive on the market stalls. At the beginning of fall, the heat of summer is fading and fresh produce perishes less easily on its way to market. Both these things contribute to make early fall a time of abundance for the organic farmer and market shopper alike. As the days become shorter and there is a chill in the air, we can enjoy the last of the summer's harvest while farmers work hard to prepare their fields for winter crops. Traditionally this was also a time when our thoughts turned to preserving, curing, and storing food for the lean and hungry winter ahead. The pumpkins sold now are not only a reminder of forthcoming Halloween, but also that we are coming to the end of something old and the beginning of something new, nature's cycle of death and rebirth.

Some foods just seem to go hand in hand with the seasons. It is difficult not to associate **mushrooms** with fall, although they can be found pretty much all year round. Cooked in a rich sauce, seasoned with fresh thyme and served with pasta or soft polenta, they make the perfect dish to cook while sipping a glass of red wine.

The humble **cauliflower**, whose numerous year-round varieties might appear to threaten its seasonal status, is still very much a fall vegetable. An organic cauliflower looks more like it would have done when it was first cultivated. It is particularly delicious at this time of year, as are the other members of the brassica family such as broccoli, sprouts, and cabbage. Organic seasonal cauliflowers are small and sweet and should be treated accordingly. Their reputation

as smelly and sulphurous is undeserved as it's only ever bad cooking that makes them so. Gently simmered in full-flavoured stock and thickened with cream and Gruyère cheese, cauliflower makes a truly indulgent, velvety soup with the texture of a rich Swiss cheese fondue.

If you've not tried **tenderstem broccoli**, now is the time to do so. This curious hybrid of broccoli and Chinese chard works perfectly with potatoes in a simple Italian-style frittata to make an ideal midweek supper for warmer days.

Pumpkins and squash are also a special treat and not just there to be carved into jack o' lanterns! Cubed and roasted, their flesh makes a great addition to a risotto along with rich Gorgonzola cheese. Or try combining pumpkin with other roasted fall vegetables, such as parsnip, in a warming red curry with just a hint of exotic Thai spice.

Silky summer-planted **leeks** are now ready to eat and plentiful. They are delicately flavored and fragrant, and make a tasty substitute for onions. Why not bake a delicious tarragon, leek, and chicken pot pie? Don't be afraid of making your own buttery pastry using organic eggs. Try it once and you won't look back. And if pies are your thing, what about a satisfying egg, bacon, and spinach version. Pies are so versatile as they are just as good served with creamy mashed potatoes as with a side salad, so they make a perfect choice during these months.

Turkey is very much a fall meat. Its flavor is enhanced in my recipe—a contemporary twist on the classic Italian saltimbocca made even tastier with the addition of aniseedy roasted **fennel**. Or try a Parmesan and herb-crumbed turkey breast served with a generous helping of creamed **spinach**. It's time for comforting classics too, like sage-crumbed pork cutlets served with Irish colcannon mash, made with the leafy and nutritious **kale**.

To make the most of fall fruits, poach ripe **pears** in Marsala and give them a classic tiramisù topping made with mascarpone cheese. For a special treat, bake a classic **apple** pie, its pastry spiced with cinnamon and warming ginger.

Try and find a small, whole head of cauliflower that is creamy-white and soft for this soup. My recipe does not involve straining the puréed mixture (a messy and laborious job) so you want to avoid cooking with a gnarly, old head for a good result. Most organic cauliflower heads are rather small. The ones you'll see at the market are what cauliflowers looked like when they were first cultivated. Although this dish is somewhere between being a soup and a fondue, it knows exactly what it is—deliciously creamy and cheesy. And it just has to be good for you with all that wonderful cauliflower in there! I have gone for a Swiss Gruyère here, keeping it well and truly within the realms of a fondue. You could add the same quantity of a sharp, aged cheddar for a "cauliflower gratin"-flavored soup or keep it light and have no cheese at all, but that wouldn't be nearly as tasty.

creamy cauliflower and Gruyère soup

2 tablespoons butter

1 onion, roughly chopped

1 celery rib, chopped

1 small cauliflower, about 2 lbs., cut into small pieces

3 quarts vegetable or chicken stock

1 cup heavy cream

2 cups grated Gruyère cheese, plus extra to serve

sea salt and freshly ground black pepper

freshly chopped parsley and toasted wholewheat bread, to serve

Serves 4

Heat the butter in a saucepan over high heat. Add the onion and celery and cook for 5 minutes, until the onion has softened but not browned.

Add the cauliflower pieces and stock and bring to a boil. Allow to boil for 25–30 minutes, until the cauliflower is really soft and breaking up in the stock.

Transfer the mixture to a food processor or blender and process the mixture in batches until smooth. Return the purée to a clean saucepan. Add the cream and cheese and cook over low heat, stirring constantly, until the cheese has all smoothly melted into the soup.

Season to taste with a little sea salt and black pepper. Serve sprinkled with chopped parsley and extra cheese and with buttered wholewheat toast on the side.

carrot and lentil soup

You'll need to use a variety of lentil here that will soften to a mush when cooked for a short time. French green lentils, or Puy, will not work. Orange or red varieties are what's needed and they also help to create the rich fall color. The taste of this soup belies the simplicity of its ingredients. Carrots can be very sweet and lentils are nutty and wholesome so they make a perfect pair. For a simple twist on this great recipe, try adding a couple of tablespoons of good-quality curry powder to the onions at the early stage of cooking.

3 tablespoons butter
1 red onion, chopped
1 garlic clove, chopped
2 tablespoons sun-dried tomato paste
1 lb. carrots, grated
1¼ cups red lentils, rinsed and drained
3 quarts chicken stock
½ cup plain yogurt
a handful of fresh cilantro, chopped

Serves 4

Heat the butter in a heavy-based saucepan over high heat. When the butter is sizzling, add the onion and garlic and cook for 4–5 minutes, stirring often. Add the sun-dried tomato paste and stir-fry for 1 minute. Add the carrots, lentils and stock to the pan and bring to the boil. Cook at a rapid simmer for 40 minutes, until the lentils are soft.

Spoon the soup, in batches, into a food processor or blender and process until smooth. Return the soup to a clean saucepan and cook over low heat for a few minutes, until heated through.

Serve with dollops of yogurt and the cilantro sprinkled on top.

spicy red vegetable soup

The color of this fiery red vegetable soup is matched by a pleasing chile kick, that can be adjusted according to your palate—just add extra chiles as required. It's a really rewarding recipe so don't be put off by the cooking time—use it as an opportunity to do a few fun chores (if there is such a thing), walk the dog or just put your feet up and relax with a glass of wine.

¼ cup light olive oil
1 tablespoon brown sugar
1 red bell pepper, chopped
2¼ lbs. Roma or plum tomatoes, quartered
1 red onion, chopped
1 large red chile, deseeded and chopped
2 garlic cloves, chopped
1 cup vegetable or chicken stock
4 slices of rye bread
2 oz. soft goat cheese

Serves 4

Preheat the oven to 350°F. Put the olive oil, sugar, bell pepper, tomatoes, onion, chile, and garlic in a roasting pan, toss everything together and cook in the preheated oven for 2 hours, stirring often, until the vegetables are really soft and starting to turn brown.

Remove the vegetables from the oven. Put the stock in a saucepan and stir in the vegetables. Spoon the mixture, in batches, into a food processor or blender and process until smooth. Return the soup to a clean saucepan and cook over low heat for a few minutes until heated through.

Toast the rye bread and, while it's still warm, spread over the cheese. Float the toast on top of the soup to serve.

The mushrooms I buy at my local market are from a mushroom farm which is housed in an abandoned railway tunnel (just one of many interesting tales I hear from passionate growers I regularly encounter.) The mushrooms thrive there, feeling right at home in the dark and dank environment. Many exotic mushroom varieties can be bought year-round, offering a constant supply of just about any mushroom you could wish for. I've used a mixture here including meaty portobello mushrooms as they go hand in hand with the other comforting, rich flavors like fresh thyme, red wine, and cinnamon.

mushroom and thyme ragu with hand-torn pasta

2 tablespoons light olive oil

2 tablespoons butter

1 onion, chopped

2 garlic cloves, chopped

3 portobello mushrooms, caps removed and cut into 1-inch pieces

6 oz. button mushrooms

3 oz. fresh shiitake mushrooms, quartered

3 fresh thyme sprigs

1 cup red wine

1 cinnamon stick

1 cup vegetable or beef stock

14 oz. fresh lasagne sheets, cut or torn into thick strips

sea salt and freshly ground black pepper

freshly grated Parmesan cheese, to serve

Serves 4

Heat the oil and butter in a heavy-based saucepan over medium heat. Add the onion and garlic and cook for 4–5 minutes, until the onions have softened. Increase the heat to high, add the mushrooms and thyme and cook for a further 8–10 minutes, stirring often, until the mushrooms darken and soften.

Add the red wine and cinnamon to the pan and boil for 5 minutes. Pour in the stock and season well with sea salt and black pepper. Reduce the heat and gently simmer the mixture for 35–40 minutes.

Cook the pasta in a saucepan of boiling water for 2–3 minutes, until it rises to the surface. Drain well and place in serving bowls. Spoon the mushroom sauce on top and sprinkle with Parmesan to serve.

Next time: Instead of serving the ragu with pasta, make the quick polenta on page 139. Spoon the mixture into a lightly oiled, medium dish, refrigerate and let cool in the dish. Cut the set polenta into your desired shapes and pan fry in a little light olive oil until golden brown on both sides. Serve the mushrooms spooned over the fried polenta.

whole-wheat pasta salad with roasted bell peppers, olives, and feta

Here, a number of typically Mediterranean flavors are served with a nutty whole-wheat pasta. Feta cheese comes in many guises and I am a big fan of most varieties, especially the creamy ones from Belgium. You may find that your local cheesemakers are making a marinated feta—soft cubes of goat feta in a herb, peppercorn, and garlic-infused olive oil. This type would work brilliantly here, adding to the salad's warm and sunny feel.

1 red bell pepper
1 yellow bell pepper
3 tablespoons light olive oil
2 teaspoons fresh thyme leaves
1 handful of flafleaf parsley, roughly chopped
1 handful of small basil leaves
2½ oz. kalamata olives, halved
14 oz. whole-wheat penne, or regular pasta
5 oz. feta cheese, crumbled
sea salt and freshly ground black pepper

Serves 4

Preheat the oven to 425°F. Brush both the bell peppers with 1 tablespoon of the oil, place in a roasting pan and cook in the preheated oven for 15 minutes, turning often until they puff up and blacken evenly all over.

Remove the bell peppers from the oven and place them in a plastic food bag. When cool enough to handle remove the skin, stalks, seeds, and any membranes and thinly slice the remaining flesh. Put the slices in a large bowl and add the remaining olive oil, herbs, and olives. Cover and set aside for 30 minutes to allow the flavors to develop.

Cook the pasta according to the packet instructions. Rinse under cold water, drain very well and add to the other ingredients. Use your hands to mix well. Season with sea salt and black pepper, add the feta and toss again before serving.

pumpkin and Gorgonzola risotto

Pumpkin gets a raw deal in some parts of the world and is generally not held in the same high regard as other members of the squash family. This isn't the case in my native Australia where pumpkin soup is almost a national dish. It's served there on cold days in large bowls and topped with dollops of sour cream and chives. Roasted pumpkin is a favorite of mine and it retains its deep flavor and unique texture here as it's roasted separately, then added to a basic risotto.

1 lb. peeled and cubed pumpkin
1 tablespoon light olive oil
1 quart vegetable stock
2 tablespoons butter
1 leek, halved lengthways and thinly sliced
1 garlic clove, chopped
1½ cups Arborio (risotto) rice
2 oz. Gorgonzola cheese, crumbled

Serves 4

Preheat the oven to 350°F.

Put the pumpkin on a baking sheet, drizzle with the olive oil and roast in the preheated oven for 30 minutes.

Put the stock in a saucepan and heat until gently simmering. Melt the butter in a saucepan over high heat and add the leek and garlic. Cook for 4–5 minutes, stirring often, until the leeks have softened but not browned.

Add the rice to the leeks and stir for 1 minute, until the rice is well coated with oil. Add ½ cup of the hot stock to the rice and cook, stirring constantly, until the rice has absorbed most of the liquid. Repeat this process until all the stock has been used, this will take about 20–25 minutes. The rice should be soft but still have a slight bite to the centre.

Add the roasted pumpkin pieces. Remove the pan from the heat, stir in the Gorgonzola and serve immediately.

See photograph on page 95.

This recipe is typical of many with an Asian influence in that most of the sauce ingredients are pantry basics. That said, I have substituted traditional Chinese black vinegar with balsamic vinegar here because it can be tricky to find. The fresh ingredients in this salad however, such as watercress, will not be hard to find but don't settle for anything less than a lovely, deep green, peppery bunch. Unfortunately, watercress does perish quite quickly so try gently wrapping your market-fresh bunch in a clean, damp kitchen towel. Stored like this in the refrigerator, it should stay fresh for a couple of days.

sesame chicken and vegetable noodle salad

2 organic chicken breasts

6 oz. dried thin egg noodles

2 tablespoons vegetable oil

2 handfuls of fresh garlic chives, snipped into 1½ inch lengths

1 leek, thinly sliced

1 small red bell pepper, deseeded and thinly sliced

1 cup bean sprouts

1 small bunch of watercress, leaves picked

1 tablespoon lightly toasted sesame seeds

sesame dressing:

2 tablespoons sesame oil

2 tablespoons light soy sauce

1 tablespoon balsamic vinegar

1 teaspoon granulated sugar

Serves 4

Preheat the oven to 350°F.

To make the dressing put the sesame oil, soy sauce, vinegar, and sugar in a small bowl and stir for a few seconds until the sugar has dissolved. Set aside until needed.

Put the chicken in a small roasting pan with ¼ cup water, cover firmly with aluminium foil and cook in the preheated oven for 30 minutes. Remove from the oven and let cool. When cool enough to handle, shred the chicken and set aside.

Cook the noodles in boiling water for 3 minutes. Rinse them under cold water to cool and drain well. Heat the vegetable oil in a frying pan over high heat. Add the chives, leeks, and red bell pepper and stir-fry for 1 minute, until the vegetables have just softened. Remove the pan from the heat and stir in the bean sprouts and watercress.

To serve, put the chicken, noodles, and vegetables in a large bowl. Add the dressing and sesame seeds and toss well.

Thai curry pastes are a staple in my kitchen. Shop around to find the ones you like but you will find that most of those made in Thailand are very good. It is a therapeutic and fun process to make your own curry paste but you will end up with a kitchen full of dried spices that, unless stored very well, will lose their intensity and have to be thrown out after a few months. The vegetables here are very earthy and distinctive, sweet and nutty and the parsnip has that delicious slightly bitter edge. Thai basil is more intensely anise flavored than other varieties. It may be hard to find so try a few leaves of fresh tarragon if you can't get hold of it. It sounds odd but the flavor works.

red curry of roasted fall vegetables

4 small new potatoes (such as Nicola or chats), halved

1 large carrot, cut into bite-sized pieces

1 tablespoon light olive oil

14 oz. pumpkin or butternut squash, peeled and cut into 1-inch pieces

1 parsnip, peeled and cut into batons

1 Spanish onion, cut into 8 wedges

1¾ cup coconut milk

2 tablespoons red curry paste

2 tablespoons brown sugar

2 tablespoons Thai fish sauce

1 cup chicken stock

a handful of fresh basil leaves (preferably Thai basil)

boiled jasmine rice, to serve

Serves 4

Preheat the oven to 425°F. Put a baking sheet in the oven for 10 minutes to heat.

Put the potatoes and carrot on the hot bakig sheet in a single layer, drizzle with the oil and roast in the preheated oven for 10 minutes. Add the pumpkin, parsnip, and onion to the sheet and roast for a further 20 minutes.

Meanwhile, put 1 cup of the coconut milk in a heavy-based saucepan and cook over high heat until at a boil. Add the curry paste and stir well. Let the mixture boil for 4–5 minutes, until the oil starts to separate from the milk. Add the sugar and fish sauce and stir-fry for 2 minutes, until the mixture is very dark.

Add the remaining coconut milk and chicken stock to the pan. Bring to a boil then stir in the roasted vegetables and the basil leaves. Cook over low heat for 5 minutes to heat through, then serve with boiled jasmine rice.

Next time: Shrimp, pumpkin, and basil make a great flavor combination. Add 20 large raw, deveined shrimp to the curry with the roasted pumpkin and basil leaves and cook over low heat for 5 minutes until the shrimp are pink, curly, and cooked through.

The frittata is Italy's version of a flat, open-faced omelet. Ideally it should be cooked slowly, only lightly colored and still slightly moist when served. My recipe flashes the frittata under the broiler to set the top. Here I am using little waxy potatoes, which are creamy and yellow and sweeter than most larger varieties, partnered with tenderstem broccoli. Part broccoli and part Chinese chard, it is one of my favorite veggies and can be added to stir-fries, pastas, and salads.

tenderstem broccoli and potato frittata

8 small waxy potatoes, quartered

1 cup vegetable stock

¼ cup light olive oil

8 oz. tenderstem or baby broccoli, trimmed and halved lengthways

1 red onion, thinly sliced

8 eggs

1 cup grated Parmesan cheese

mixed green salad, to serve

Serves 4

Put the potatoes in a large nonstick frying pan and pour over the stock. Put the pan over high heat and bring the stock to a boil. Boil for 10 minutes, turning the potatoes often, until almost all the stock has been absorbed.

Add the olive oil, broccoli, and onion to the pan and cook for 1 minute, turning the vegetables to coat in the oil. Cover and cook for 2–3 minutes, to soften the broccoli.

Preheat the broiler to high. Lightly beat the eggs with half of the Parmesan and pour over the vegetables. Cover the pan and cook over medium heat for 8–10 minutes, until the eggs look set.

Sprinkle over the remaining cheese, then place under the preheated broiler and cook until the top of the frittata is golden. Let cool slightly before removing from the pan. Cut into wedges and serve with a mixed green salad.

Next time: Add 3½ oz. diced pancetta (Italian cured bacon) to the pan with the potatoes, allowing it to impart its mildly spiced and peppery flavor. Or, staying with a vegetarian version, top the frittata with 3½ oz. strong-flavored cheese, such as fontina, just before putting it under the hot broiler, so that it melts and gives the frittata a gooey and golden topping.

Fall is a great time for pies. Typically the weather is fickle and with a pie you have the option of serving a slice with creamy mashed potato if it's chilly or with a salad of late season tomatoes and a tangy dressing if the days are still warm. Pies are also as good outdoors as they are indoors. They transport well for picnics and leftovers will sit happily in the fridge for a couple of days so you can enjoy them as a snack or late supper.

egg, bacon, and spinach pie

1 lb. fresh spinach

1 tablespoon butter

3 slices rindless bacon, cut into thin strips

1 onion, finely chopped

6 eggs, lightly beaten

½ cup finely grated Parmesan cheese

1 egg, lightly beaten with 1 tablespoon cold water

shortcrust pastry:

2 cups all-purpose flour

1 stick plus 2 tablespoons butter, cut into small cubes

1 egg yolk

a loose-based tart pan, 8 inches across, lightly greased

Serves 6

Put the flour and butter into the bowl of a food processor and put the bowl into the freezer for 15 minutes. Lightly beat the egg yolk with 2 tablespoons water and refrigerate for 15 minutes. Process the butter and flour until the mixture looks like ground almonds, then add the egg yolk mixture and process for just a few seconds to combine. Tip the mixture into a bowl and use your hands to bring the dough together to form one large ball. It should be a bit crumbly. Wrap in plastic wrap and refrigerate for 30 minutes.

Preheat the oven to 350°F. Wash the spinach and, leaving some of the water on the leaves, cook it in a large nonstick frying pan over high heat for 2 minutes, until wilted and emerald green in color. You may need to cook the spinach in batches. Transfer it to a colander and drain well. When cool enough to handle, use your hands to squeeze out as much moisture as possible from the spinach and place it in a large bowl.

Heat the butter in the frying pan over high heat and, when sizzling, add the bacon and onion. Cook for 5 minutes until golden. Spoon the mixture into the bowl with the spinach. Add the eggs and Parmesan and season well with sea salt and black pepper. Stir to combine.

Put the greased tart pan on a baking sheet. Cut about two-thirds from the ball of dough and roll it out between two layers of wax paper. Line the bottom of the tart pan with the pastry. Spoon the spinach mixture on top of the pastry base. Roll the remaining pastry into a circle slightly larger than the tart pan and place this on top of the pie, allowing any excess pastry to hang over the edge. Gently press down around the edges to seal. Brush the egg and water mixture over the pie and cook in the preheated oven for 1 hour until golden brown.

Let the pie cool for 10–15 minutes before cutting into wedges to serve.

When fall really sets in it is good to know you can rely on one shining beacon of fresh-grown produce: the leek. While most other vegetables are waiting for spring to make it to the dinner table again, summer-planted leeks will be ready to enjoy long after the summer has gone. Parsley, chives, chervil, and tarragon make up the *fines herbes* of French cooking. These herbs really like being in a dish throughout the entire cooking process, unlike the bouquet garni herbs which are removed during cooking. Do look out for anise-flavored fresh tarragon as it's particularly good with chicken and cream. I have included a pastry recipe which isn't as intimidating as it looks so do try it at least once before resorting to frozen pastry.

tarragon, chicken, and leek pot pie

3 tablespoons butter

1½ lbs. boneless, skinless organic chicken thighs, cut into bite-sized pieces

4 medium leeks (white parts only), thickly sliced

3 tablespoons all-purpose flour

1 cup chicken stock

1 cup light cream

2 tablespoons finely chopped fresh tarragon

2 tablespoons roughly chopped flat leaf parsley

sea salt and freshly ground black pepper

pie pastry:

1½ cups all-purpose flour

2 tablespoons butter

2 tablespoons sour cream

1 egg, lightly beaten

3 quart capacity ovenproof pie dish

Serves 4

Heat half of the butter in a frying pan over high heat. When the butter is sizzling, cook the chicken in two batches for 2–3 minutes, turning often so that the pieces are browned all over. Transfer to a bowl.

Add the remaining butter to the pan and cook the leeks over medium heat for 2 minutes. Cover with a lid, reduce the heat, and cook for 2–3 minutes, until really softened.

Return the chicken to the pan and increase the heat to high. Sprinkle the flour into the pan and cook for 2 minutes, stirring constantly so that the flour thickly coats the chicken and leeks. Gradually add the chicken stock, stirring all the time. Bring to a boil, then stir in the cream, tarragon, and parsley. Season well. Reduce heat and simmer until thickened, about 1 minute. Remove from the heat and let cool. Spoon into an ovenproof pie dish.

To make the pastry, put the flour, butter, and a pinch of salt in a food processor and process for a few seconds. With the motor running, add the sour cream, half of the beaten egg and add 1–2 tablespoons cold water, until the dough comes together. Roll into a ball, wrap in plastic wrap, and refrigerate for 30 minutes.

Preheat the oven to 350°F. Place the dough between two pieces of wax paper and roll out to a thickness of ¼ inch, making sure the dough is more than big enough to cover the dish. Fold the dough over the top of the pie, leaving the edges to overhang. Cut several slits in the top of the pie and gently press around the edges with a fork. Brush the remaining beaten egg over the top. Put the pie dish on a baking sheet and cook in the preheated oven for 30 minutes, until the pastry is golden.

I was so excited when I found a supplier of locally farmed organic turkeys. These turkeys were able to grow up in an environment that only the great outdoors can provide: sunshine, pasture, and lots of room to run around. Many of these farms will also take orders for Thanksgiving birds, or just parts of the bird, like the breast I have used here. This recipe is good news for those of you who feel turkey can be disappointing. The juicy, lean, full-flavored meat is made even tastier when coated in Parmesan-flavored crumbs and pan-fried until beautifully golden. The creamed spinach isn't bad either!

Parmesan and herb crumbed turkey with creamed spinach

1 cup all-purpose flour

2 eggs

1½ cups grated Parmesan cheese

1½ cups fresh breadcrumbs

1 teaspoon finely chopped fresh thyme

2 large organic turkey breasts, about 14 oz. each

½ cup light olive oil

lemon wedges, to serve (optional)

creamed spinach:

2 bunches spinach (about 16 oz.), stalks trimmed and roughly chopped

2 tablespoons heavy cream

a pinch of grated nutmeg

sea salt

Serves 4

Put the flour on a plate. Put the eggs in a bowl and lightly beat with 2 tablespoons water. In a separate bowl, mix the Parmesan, breadcrumbs, and thyme. Toss each turkey breast in the flour to coat, then dip in the egg and finally in the Parmesan crumb mixture, pressing down to evenly coat in the crumbs. Transfer to a plate, cover, and refrigerate until needed.

To make the creamed spinach, wash the spinach thoroughly and do not shake dry. Put the spinach in a saucepan with the water still clinging to the leaves, cover with a lid and cook over medium heat for 2–3 minutes, stirring the leaves so they wilt and soften. Transfer the spinach to a food processor. Add the cream and nutmeg and season well with sea salt. Process until smooth. Return the spinach to a clean saucepan and keep warm until ready to serve.

Preheat the oven to 350°F. Heat the olive oil in a frying pan over high heat. When the oil is hot, but not smoking, add the turkey and cook for 3–4 minutes on each side until a golden crust is formed. Put the turkey on a baking sheet and cook in the preheated oven for 10 minutes.

To serve, cut the turkey into thick slices and serve with creamed spinach and lemon wedges on the side to squeeze over, if you like.

In fall it shouldn't be too hard to find a supplier who will guarantee that the turkey you buy has had a free-range life, full of pecking, flapping, and scratching around in the dirt, before it gets to your table. The same cannot be said of veal, which is the cut of meat traditionally used in an Italian-style *saltimbocca*. Thin slices of turkey breast don't need much cooking time so they work well in my alternative recipe. The cream and fennel are a pretty good flavor combination and really complement the turkey in this classic dish with a twist.

turkey saltimbocca with roasted fennel

4 turkey breast fillets, about 4 oz. each

½ cup all-purpose flour

a pinch of salt

a pinch of ground white pepper

8 thin slices of prosciutto or parma ham

8 fresh sage leaves

4 small fennel bulbs, cut into wedges and fronds finely chopped

3 tablespoons light olive oil

freshly squeezed juice of 1 lemon

3 tablespoons butter

½ cup Marsala or brandy

½ cup light cream

½ cup freshly shelled peas

sea salt and freshly ground black pepper

Serves 4

Preheat the oven to 350°F.

Cut the turkey fillets in half lengthways. Place a piece of turkey between two pieces of plastic wrap and gently pound with a meat mallet until the turkey has a thickness of ¼ inch. Repeat this process to make 8 thin fillets.

Put the flour on a plate and add a pinch of salt and a pinch of white pepper. Press each piece of turkey onto the flour to evenly coat. Wrap 1 slice of prosciutto around each piece of turkey and place 2 sage leaves onto the prosciutto. Set aside.

Put the fennel in a small roasting pan with 2 tablespoons of the olive oil and half of the lemon juice. Toss to coat the fennel in the oil mixture and roast in the preheated oven for 40 minutes, turning often until soft and golden. Remove from the oven and set aside while you cook the turkey.

Heat the butter and remaining 1 tablespoon of olive oil in a large frying pan over high heat. When the butter is sizzling, add the turkey, sage side-down, and cook for 2 minutes. Turn over and cook for a further 2 minutes. Add the Marsala or brandy to the pan, shaking the pan, and cook for 1 minute.

Transfer the turkey to a serving plate, leaving the liquid in the pan. Add the cooked fennel, cream, peas, and remaining lemon juice to the pan and cook for 3–4 minutes, stirring well to incorporate any of the stuck on bits, until the sauce thickens and coats the fennel. Season the sauce with sea salt and black pepper.

Spoon the sauce and fennel over the turkey and serve.

It's easy to forget that meat was once a seasonal treat. Pigs were fattened up by eating the leftovers of the land, such as windfall apples. Easy to prepare, these sage-crumbed pork chops are served here with Irish-style colcannon. This is comfort food at its best—a creamy mashed potato with cooked cabbage. My colcannon recipe uses kale, a close relative of the cabbage. You may also see the trendy black variety, known as *cavolo nero,* popping its head up in all the cool eateries. This is a true cold weather vegetable that actually relies on frost to enhance its flavor. So as the weather gets colder, the kale gets better, making it the perfect choice for late fall.

sage pork chops with kale colcannon

½ cup all-purpose flour

3 eggs

2 tablespoons Worcestershire sauce

4–6 fresh sage leaves, finely chopped

1 cup fresh breadcrumbs

1 cup finely grated Parmesan cheese

4 pork chops

¼ cup vegetable oil

kale colcannon:

1 lb. curly kale

2 tablespoons butter

2 slices of bacon, cut into strips

6–8 scallions, thinly sliced

4 large potatoes, quartered

1 stick butter, cut into cubes

Serves 4

Put the all-purpose flour on a large, flat plate. Mix the eggs and Worcestershire sauce in a bowl and, in a separate bowl, combine the sage, breadcrumbs, and Parmesan. Press a pork chop into the flour, coating the meat evenly, then dip it in the egg mixture, then press firmly to coat in the crumb mix. Repeat this process with all 4 pork chops. Transfer them to a plate and refrigerate until needed.

To make the colcannon, cook the kale in a large saucepan of boiling water for 5 minutes. Drain well, chop finely, and set aside.

Put the 2 tablespoons of butter in a frying pan over medium heat. Add the bacon and cook for 5 minutes, stirring occasionally until the bacon turns golden. Add the scallions and cook for a further 2 minutes. Stir in the kale and remove the pan from the heat.

Put the potatoes in a large saucepan and cover with cold water. Bring to a boil and cook for 20 minutes, until soft when pierced with a skewer but not breaking apart. Drain the potatoes well and return them to the pan. Add the butter and mash well. Beat with a wooden spoon until smooth. Stir the kale mixture into the potatoes, cover, and keep warm while cooking the pork.

Heat the vegetable oil in a large frying pan over medium heat. When hot, add the pork chops and cook for 6–7 minutes, so they gently sizzle in the oil and a golden crust forms. Turn over the pork chops and cook for 5 minutes on the other side. Serve with a generous portion of the kale colcannon.

fig and honey croissant pudding

These soft, pear-shaped fruits have a sweet, honey-nectar flavor that is lovely with cured meats and cheese. Once picked, they ripen very quickly and late-season figs are perfect cooked in puddings or savored with cheese.

2 croissants, preferably stale, each torn into 6 pieces
6 fresh figs, halved
¼ cup honey
3 eggs
1 cup whole milk
1 cup light cream
¼ cup granulated sugar
heavy cream, to serve

a medium baking dish, lightly greased

Serves 4

Preheat the oven to 350°F.

Put the croissant pieces in the bottom of the greased dish. Arrange the fig halves in between the croissant pieces and drizzle the honey over the top.

Combine the eggs, milk, cream, and sugar in a bowl and pour into the dish. Let stand for about 20 minutes so that the croissants can absorb some of the custard. Bake in the preheated oven for 50 minutes, until the top of the pudding is a dark golden brown.

Let cool a little before cutting into slices and serving with dollops of heavy cream on the side.

Next time: When figs aren't in season, you can lightly spread each piece of croissant with some good-quality fig jelly before putting into the dish. Leave out the honey and add ⅓ cup slivered almonds to the egg mixture instead.

See photograph on page 113.

almond and blood orange syrup cake

I once heard a blood orange described as "an orange which has been kissed by a raspberry." How true! They have that sherberty orange flavor with hints of raspberry and a divine color, but no one really seems to know why they are the color they are. The fact that they are a truly seasonal fruit, available only for a few months from late fall, makes them even more special to cook with.

1½ cups blanched almonds
1 cup plus 2 tablespoons granulated sugar
6 tablespoons self-rising flour
2 sticks unsalted butter, at room temperature
1 tablespoon grated blood orange zest
4 eggs
½ cup flaked almonds, lightly toasted
heavy cream, to serve

blood orange syrup:
¼ cup freshly squeezed blood orange juice
¼ cup granulated sugar

a springform cake pan, 9 inches across, lightly greased

Serves 8

Preheat the oven to 350°F.

Put the almonds in a food processor and process until finely chopped. Transfer them to a bowl and mix in the sugar and flour.

Beat the butter and zest for 1 minute, then add the eggs, one at a time, beating well after each addition until well mixed. Add the almond, and flour mixture in 2 batches and beat again until well combined. Spoon into the prepared cake pan. Bake in the preheated oven for 45 minutes, until golden on top. Remove the cake from the oven and prick it all over with a skewer.

To make the syrup, put the blood orange juice and sugar in a small saucepan over high heat, stirring until the sugar has dissolved. As soon as the mixture comes to a boil remove the pan from the heat and pour the syrup over the cake.

Let the cake cool in the pan then sprinkle the flaked almonds on top. Slice and serve with extra thick double cream on the side.

These are a cheat's delight—so simple and quick to make and deliciously fresh-tasting. I use Red Delicious apples in early fall at a time when blueberries are in their last few weeks. Both fruits are perfect to cook with and just lovely with vanilla. Any leftover tarts can be served cold and enjoyed with coffee the next day. Just dust them with some confectioners' sugar and eat them as you would a fruit-filled Danish pastry.

apple and blueberry tarts

12-oz. sheet ready-rolled puff pastry dough, defrosted if frozen, cut into 4 squares each about 5 inches square

2 tablespoons granulated sugar

1 vanilla bean, cut in half lengthways

3 sweet dessert apples (such as Red Delicious or Braeburn), each cored and cut into 10–12 thin wedges

1 basket blueberries

heavy cream, to serve

a baking sheet lined with baking paper

Serves 4

Preheat the oven to 425°F.

Place the puff pastry squares on a lined baking sheet.

Put the sugar and 2 tablespoons of water in a saucepan and bring to a boil, stirring until the sugar dissolves. Scrape the seeds from the vanilla directly into the sugar syrup, stirring to combine.

Add the apple slices to the pan, reduce the heat to medium and cook for 4–5 minutes, turning the apples so they cook evenly. Add the blueberries and gently stir to coat in the sweet syrup. Arrange the apples and blueberries on top of each pastry square. Bake in the preheated oven for 18–20 minutes, until the pastry is puffed and golden.

Serve warm with the cream spooned over the top.

Next time: For a simple French-style apple frangipane tart, mix 2 tablespoons each of room temperature butter, ground almonds and icing sugar with 1 tablespoon all-purpose flour in a bowl until you have a paste. Stir in 1 egg yolk until smooth. Spread the mixture over each of the pastry squares, leaving a space around the edge, and top with the apple slices. Bake in a preheated oven at 425°F for 18–20 minutes, until puffed and golden. This tart can also be topped with poached pears (see page 121), drained of excess liquid.

The inspiration for this recipe came from my oldest cookbook, whose once cream-colored dust jacket is now as dusky as the spice-filled pastry in this recipe. Rolling this rustic and crumbly pastry and filling it with lemon-infused apples is a very organic process you will want to enjoy again and again, just as I have...

dusky apple pie

8 tart green apples (such as Granny Smith), peeled, cored and thinly sliced

2 teaspoons freshly squeezed lemon juice

2 thin slices of lemon zest

¼ cup granulated sugar

2 cups self-rising flour

¾ cups packed brown sugar

1 tablespoon ground cinnamon

1 tablespoon ground ginger

1 stick cold butter, cut into cubes

1 egg, lightly beaten

vanilla ice cream, to serve (optional)

a loose-based fluted tart tin, 8 x 1½ inches high, lightly greased

Serves 8–10

Put the apple slices in a saucepan with the lemon juice, lemon zest, and sugar. Cover and cook over low heat for 15–20 minutes, turning the apples often so they soften and cook evenly. Set aside and let cool.

To make the pastry, put the flour, brown sugar, and spices in a food processor and process for a few seconds to combine. With the motor running, add the butter several cubes at a time. Add the egg and 1–2 tablespoons of cold water and process until combined. The dough will look dry and crumbly. Transfer to a bowl and knead to form a ball. Wrap the ball in plastic wrap and refrigerate for 30 minutes.

Preheat the oven to 350°F and put a baking sheet in the oven to heat up. Cut the dough into two portions, with one slightly larger than the other. Roll the larger piece of dough between two sheets of wax paper and use it to line the bottom and sides of the prepared tart tin. (Take care when handling the pastry as it will be quite crumbly.) Trim the edge of the pastry to fit the tin.

Spoon the apples on top of the pastry base. Roll the remaining pastry to a circle large enough to cover the base and place on top of the pie, trimming the edges to fit. Use a small sharp knife to make several slits in the pastry. Put the pie on the hot baking sheet and bake in the preheated oven for 50–55 minutes, until the pastry is dark brown.

Remove the pie from the oven and let it rest for 15–20 minutes before cutting into wedges and serving with vanilla ice cream on the side.

I wonder if tiramisù (which literally translates from the Italian as pick-me-up) is one of the best-loved desserts in the world. It has all the essential elements of a perfect sweet—alcohol, creamy custard, and cocoa. Pears work particularly well with anything sweet, creamy, and cheesey so mascarpone makes an ideal partner. Do choose your pears carefully. Soft and sweet varieties do not poach well and will end up as an overly sweet mush. Bosc are good, but any market-fresh firm, brown variety will work in this lovely recipe.

poached pear tiramisù

6–8 ladyfinger cookies (Italian savoiardi)

1 cup Marsala or brandy

½ cup plus 1 tablespoon granulated sugar

2 firm brown pears (such as Bosc), peeled, cored and cut into eighths

2 egg whites

4 egg yolks

1 cup mascarpone cheese

cocoa powder, for dusting

4 individual serving dishes

Serves 6

Line the bottom of each serving dish with sponge fingers, breaking them in order to fit them in.

Put the Marsala or brandy, half of the sugar and ½ cup water in a nonstick frying pan and cook over high heat until the mixture comes to a boil, stirring until the sugar has dissolved. Add the pears and cook on a gentle simmer for 20 minutes, turning them often until they are soft and glossy and there is about half of the liquid remaining.

Lay the pears on top of the ladyfingers and pour over the poaching liquid. Using electric beaters, beat the egg whites until firm peaks form. Beat the egg yolks with the remaining sugar for 4–5 minutes, until they are pale in color and doubled in size, then beat the mascarpone into the yolks until smooth.

Using a large spoon, fold the egg whites into the yolk and sugar mixture and spoon this over the pears. Cover each dish with plastic wrap and refrigerate until ready to serve.

Dust each one with a little cocoa powder just before serving.

winter

the tastes of **winter**

The lack of daylight and colder weather can make winter a gloomy time of year, so it's not surprising that we seek comfort from our food. The trees may be bare but your kitchen need not be. It's time to batten down the hatches, stay inside in the warm and really enjoy some cooking. Winter cooking need not mean hours of work preparing ingredients either, as its the time of year when slow cooking really comes into it's own. Food should be all about one-pot wonders such as hearty soups, stews, and casseroles. Ideally it should be about putting a selection of carefully chosen ingredients in a pot, sitting back and letting the alchemy of cooking do the rest. There is nothing quite like lifting the lid of a casserole at the table and releasing the delicious, mouth-watering aromas of the food within.

Unlike the spring cook, the winter cook is not required to be particularly creative as there is an abundance of great winter produce to work with. Winter vegetables become the star attraction in the kitchen now, with a side show of organic meat and well-chosen accompaniments. Root vegetables such as turnips, parsnips, beet, celeriac, carrots, and sweet potatoes may be out of sight under the ground but they are certainly not out of mind. They are nutritious and delicious and seem to have been custom-made to see us through these colder months.

I've combined three of these heavyweight root veggies, **parsnip, turnip, and sweet potato**, in a fruity and exotic Moroccan-style tagine, served with fluffy couscous. If you've never tried **Swiss chard** now is the season to do so. Similar to spinach, but with a stronger, more robust flavour, it makes is an ideal addition to hearty winter soups. I use it in a satisfying minestrone that is packed with creamy cannellini beans and topped with generous amounts of freshly grated Parmesan. **Brussels sprouts** are also a seasonal treat. They may look very much like baby cabbages but they have a completely unique nutty yet sweet flavour. They have a natural affinity with **chestnuts**, also widely available in winter, and slow-cooked together in stock with a little pancetta, the Italian salt-cured bacon, they make a delicious side dish to serve with any roast.

Beans and lentils are an essential ingredient in winter cooking too. Buy them canned or dried and use in a wide variety of dishes. A sustaining soup is easily made with chickpeas, aniseedy fennel, and chopped cured bacon. **Grains and rice** are also a useful staple. Try sweet roasted baby carrots in a simple risotto made with barley or my interpretation of a traditional Scotch broth, made with nutritious and wholesome brown rice.

If you've become a bit of a couch potato and feel the need for something lighter to eat, then the winter markets will still provide plenty of vegetables that work well in a salad. A winter coleslaw made with shredded **celeriac**, cabbage, and carrots, spiced up with red chiles and a Vietnamese-style dressing, is perfect served in a sandwich with some chicken. Any winter salad greens can be turned into something special with a little imagination. Try a **beet**, pecan and goat cheese salad or combine Belgian endive and chicory leaves with slices of crisp cold weather **pears** and a full-flavored blue cheese, such as Gorgonzola.

At one time meat was a weekly treat, usually reserved for Sundays when it was roasted and served with all the trimmings. Even though meat is available to us all year round, winter is still a time of year for lovers of organic meat to rejoice. Your local butcher or farmers' market is sure to know a local **organic sausage** maker. Find a variety you particularly enjoy, my current favorite is a pork and fennel one. Cook it in a smoky sausage and bean casserole or serve it with a crispy, pan-fried **potato** and celeriac rösti. If you enjoy a big meat centerpiece, serve a pork roast alongside a helping of savory apple and **fennel** pudding. For a special occasion, try braising premium beef fillet in red wine or roasting it and serving with roasted winter vegetables and a rich garlic crème. Either is perfect accompanied with crisp little "smashed" roasted potatoes, cooked hot and fast to give them light fluffy centers and crisp skins—just the way I like them.

Dark, bittersweet chocolate is the perfect pick-me-up on gloomier days and I guarantee my recipe for a chocolate orange mousse, rich with Grand Marnier, won't disappoint.

winter coleslaw and chicken salad sandwich

2 cups finely shredded celeriac

1½ cups finely shredded Chinese cabbage

1 carrot, peeled and cut into julienne strips

2 celery ribs, thinly sliced on the angle

1 small bunch of cilantro, leaves and stems roughly chopped

1 large handful of fresh mint leaves, chopped

½ rotisserie chicken, meat and skin shredded

1 long French baguette

mayonnaise, to serve

Vietnamese dressing:

3 tablespoons Thai fish sauce

2 tablespoons rice vinegar

freshly squeezed juice of 1 lemon

1 large red chile, deseeded and finely chopped

1 teaspoon sugar

Serves 2

If you are craving a salad in winter, then you cannot beat a good coleslaw that makes use of abundant cold-weather veggies. I have used an exotic Chinese cabbage here but savoy will do the trick. The salad itself will be just fine with traditional mayonnaise but I love the flavors of this Vietnamese dressing. You could serve this in a baguette, like they do in Vietnam, and the crisp fresh flavors will transport you to a Saigon café.

To make the dressing, put all the ingredients in a small bowl and stir for a few seconds to dissolve the sugar. Set aside until needed.

Put all the vegetables, herbs, and shredded chicken in a large bowl and toss to mix. Add the dressing and toss again. To serve, cut the baguette in half and then slice each piece in half lengthways in order to make a sandwich.

Spread each piece of bread with the desired quantity of mayonnaise and fill with the chicken salad.

Belgian endive, pear, and Gorgonzola salad

Belgian endive comes from a large family, all descended from European wild chicory, each with varying levels of bitterness. It is usually white but can be purple. This salad will work just as well using the other bitter endive cousins, such as radicchio and frisée. Sweet pear balances the bitter greens in this salad and we already know how well pears and cheese go together.

½ cup walnuts, lightly toasted and roughly chopped

1 small green Belgian endive, leaves separated

1 small purple Belgian endive, leaves separated

4 large handfuls of baby spinach

2 firm pears (such as Bosc), cored and cut into thin wedges

3½ oz. Gorgonzola cheese

orange mustard dressing:
freshly squeezed juice of 1 orange

½ cup light olive oil

2 teaspoons Dijon mustard

1 tablespoon red wine vinegar

Serves 4, as a starter

To make the dressing, put the orange juice, olive oil, mustard, and vinegar in a small bowl and mix well. Cover and set aside.

Put the walnuts, endive, spinach, and pear in a large bowl and toss to mix. Transfer to a serving plate, crumble the cheese on top and spoon over the dressing to serve.

Next time: A simple variation on this recipe makes the perfect winter duck salad. Prepare the salad without the cheese. Broil 2 duck breasts to your liking. Allow them to rest for 10 minutes to tenderize, then slice each once across the breast into ½-inch wide strips. Add the duck to the other ingredients, including the dressing and toss to mix. The flavor of duck works well with all the other flavors: pears, oranges, walnuts, and even the mustard in the dressing.

beet, pecan, and goat cheese salad with maple dressing

There was a time when beet was overlooked in favour of its pretty purple leaves. Thankfully we've now come to appreciate the sweet, purple root of the beet. It can be roasted in its skin, puréed for a dip or spread, or grated raw as a fresh and vibrant addition to a winter salad. It's just lovely with soft goat cheese and nuts, and works well with other sweet flavors such as honey, brown sugar, sweet mustards, or pomegranate molasses—the distinctive Middle Eastern sweet-yet-tart syrup.

4 medium beets

2 large handfuls of small beet leaves

2 large handfuls of wild arugula

⅔ cup pecan nuts, lightly toasted and roughly chopped

1 bunch of chives, snipped

5 oz. firm goat cheese

maple dressing:
2 tablespoons pure maple syrup

3 tablespoons extra virgin olive oil

2 tablespoons white wine vinegar

1 teaspoon wholegrain mustard

freshly ground black pepper

Serves 4, as a starter

To make the dressing, combine all the ingredients in a small bowl with some freshly ground black pepper and set aside to allow the flavors to develop.

Preheat the oven to 350°F. Put the beets in a small roasting pan with 1 cup water. Cover the pan with aluminium foil and cook in the preheated oven for 1 hour.

Remove the pan from the oven and, leaving the pan covered, let the beets cool. Peel the beets and cut each one into eighths. Put it in a large bowl with the beet leaves, arugula, pecans, chives, and half of the maple dressing. Toss well and transfer to a serving plate.

Crumble the goat cheese over the salad, pour over the remaining dressing and serve.

See photograph on page 131.

Swiss chard and white bean minestrone

Minestrone is a style of delicious Italian vegetable soup that can really be whatever you want it to be. It can be fancy and complex or laid back and unpretentious, like this recipe. The soup is beefed up here by serving ladles of the hot minestrone over thick and garlicky toasted ciabatta to mop up all the goodness.

2 tablespoons butter

1 onion, chopped

1 small bunch of Swiss chard (12 oz.), finely chopped

1 quart vegetable stock

14 oz. canned cannellini beans, drained but not rinsed and roughly mashed

4 thick slices of ciabatta

2 garlic cloves, halved

extra virgin olive oil, for drizzling

finely grated Parmesan cheese, to serve

sea salt and freshly ground black pepper

Serves 4

Melt the butter in a saucepan over medium heat. Add the onion and cook for 4–5 minutes to soften. Add the Swiss chard and cook for 5 minutes, stirring often, until softened. Add the stock and beans and gently bring to a boil. Season with sea salt and black pepper.

Toast the ciabatta until golden on both sides. Rub the bread with the cut side of the garlic, then place each one in a serving bowl. Drizzle each piece of bread with olive oil and ladle over the soup. Sprinkle the Parmesan on top and serve immediately.

Next time: It's easy to turn this into a satisfying pasta meal. Simply leave out the stock and add 14 oz. cooked pasta shapes to the pan when you add the beans, season well with sea salt and black pepper and stir in some finely grated Parmesan cheese for extra flavor.

This version of a minestrone is really a meal in its own right. It's packed with lovely winter vegetables and is a "one-pot wonder" that will improve with age. I consider pancetta, the cured Italian bacon, to be an essential ingredient that should be on hand in every kitchen. It comes in a sausage-like roll or ready chopped and pre-packed and is slightly salty but bursting with intense flavors, like garlic and pepper.

chunky chickpea soup

2 tablespoons olive oil

1 leek, thinly sliced

1 small fennel bulb, cut into small dice

3½ oz. pancetta, cut into small cubes

1 carrot, grated

1 potato, cut into small cubes

3 quarts chicken stock

14 oz. canned chickpeas, rinsed and drained

3 oz. fresh spinach, chopped

½ cup finely grated Parmesan cheese

sea salt and freshly ground black pepper

Serves 4

Heat the oil in a saucepan. Add the leek, fennel, and pancetta and cook for 5 minutes over high heat, until the leek softens and the pancetta really flavors the oil. Add the carrot, potato, stock, and chickpeas and bring to a boil.

Reduce the heat and simmer for 20 minutes. Season to taste with sea salt and black pepper then add the spinach. Cook over low heat for 5 minutes, until the spinach has wilted throughout the soup.

Serve with Parmesan sprinkled over the top.

Next time: Add 3½ oz. small pasta (try the little rice-shaped pastas such as risoni or orzo) instead of chickpeas and simmer until the pasta is cooked through before adding the final few ingredients. This will give you a very thick soup that you may even need a fork to eat!

Scotch broth

2 tablespoons light olive oil

1 carrot, diced

1 leek, diced

2 celery ribs, diced and leaves chopped

1 lb. stewing lamb, well trimmed of fat and cubed

2 cups chicken stock

1 tablespoon light soy sauce

½ cup brown rice

sea salt and freshly ground black pepper

4 soft dinner rolls, buttered, to serve

Serves 4

From the land that brings us haggis, kippers, neeps, and tatties comes its famous namesake broth. Barley is traditionally used, but I have substituted it with brown rice. I am fairly certain that soy sauce is never used in traditional Scottish fare but it works well with the other flavors in this recipe. I have kept this dead simple with a minimum of ingredients but you could add some herbs if you like. Thyme, in particular, likes being with lamb.

Heat the oil in a large saucepan. Add the carrot, leek, celery stalks, and leaves and cook over high heat for 5 minutes, stirring often. Add the lamb, stock, soy sauce, rice, and 1 quart of water and bring to a boil.

Reduce the heat to low, cover with a tight-fitting lid and let the soup simmer for 1 hour. Season to taste with sea salt and black pepper and serve with the soft, buttered rolls on the side.

broccoli, garlic, and spinach with Parmesan polenta

Broccoli provides us with a bumper supply of vitamin C in the colder months and is loaded with fiber. It's versatile too—just as much at home in an Asian stir-fry as it is in a quick pasta dish. Combined with spinach here, it makes a tasty sauce that could be served with a spiral or tube-shaped pasta but I have chosen a quick-cook polenta. This basic recipe makes an equally delicious side to the Roasted Spring Chicken (see page 35) or the Red Wine Braised Beef (see page 153).

14 oz. broccoli, sliced into thin wedges
2 garlic cloves, thinly sliced
1 cup chicken stock
¼ cup light olive oil
3½ cups baby spinach
freshly grated Parmesan cheese, to serve

Parmesan polenta:
2 cups milk
1 cup instant polenta
5 tablespoons butter
1 cup grated Parmesan cheese
sea salt and freshly ground black pepper

Serves 4

Put the broccoli, garlic, stock, and oil in a frying pan, cover the pan and cook over high heat for 10 minutes, turning the broccoli often, until there is only a few tablespoons of stock left in the pan. Add the spinach and cook over medium heat for 2–3 minutes, stirring often until the spinach has wilted and is combined with the broccoli. Cover and set aside while you cook the polenta.

To make the Parmesan polenta, put the milk in a saucepan with 1 quart water. Cook over medium heat until simmering, then slowly pour in the polenta in a steady stream, using a whisk to combine. Reduce the heat to low and cook for 5 minutes, stirring constantly with a wooden spoon, until the polenta grains are soft. Add the butter and Parmesan and remove the pan from the heat. Stir until the butter and Parmesan are smoothly incorporated in the polenta and season well with sea salt and black pepper. Spoon onto serving plates.

Quickly reheat the broccoli mixture and spoon over the polenta. Sprinkle extra Parmesan on top to serve.

roasted carrots with barley risotto

Barley is a wonderful ingredient—it's so earthy and unprocessed and I like to throw it into all sort of things, such as lamb stews and soups. I've used it here to make a dish much like a risotto, but without all the stirring! Despite seeming an odd couple, miso and Parmesan do work well together and give the barley an intensely savory flavor that's perfect with sweet carrots.

2 tablespoons light olive oil
12 baby carrots, ends trimmed
2 tablespoons butter
2 sprigs of fresh thyme
2 garlic cloves, unpeeled and cut in half
2 cups chicken stock
1 tablespoon light soy sauce
1¼ cups pearl barley
1 tablespoon butter
3 heaped tablespoons finely grated Parmesan cheese
sea salt and freshly ground black pepper

Serves 4

Heat the oil in a frying pan until very hot. Add the carrots and cook for 8–10 minutes, turning every 2 minutes, until golden. If your pan isn't big enough you may need to do this in batches. Add the butter, thyme, and garlic to the pan with ½ cup water and season with sea salt and black pepper. Cover the pan with a tight-fitting lid and cook over medium heat for 15–20 minutes, turning often, until the carrots are tender.

Meanwhile, to make the barley risotto, put the stock and soy sauce in a saucepan with 1 quart water and bring to a boil. Add the barley and cook for 45–50 minutes, stirring often, until the barley is soft but not breaking up. Stir in the butter and Parmesan. Serve the carrots on top of the barley.

Next time: The carrots could be served hot on a bed of couscous or, left to cool and tossed in a salad with beets, toasted pine nuts, and a soft cheese. They are also perfect when roughly chopped and added to the risotto recipe on page 93, in place of the roasted pumpkin.

See photograph on page 141.

Although it sounds rather exotic, a tagine is really nothing more than a stew. It gets its name from the conical, lidded, earthenware cooking dish traditionally used in Morocco. It really can have just about anything you like in it, provided there are the obligatory fragrant and aromatic spices, so typical of Moroccan cooking. It's these rather heavy, pungent spices that go so well with the full-flavored winter vegetables I have used here. They all grow underground so I couldn't resist giving them a breath of air by throwing in some crisp apples and fresh mint.

winter vegetable tagine

3 tablespoons light olive oil

1 onion, chopped

2 garlic cloves, chopped

½ teaspoon turmeric

½ teaspoon paprika

1 teaspoon ground cumin

1 cinnamon stick

14 oz. canned chopped tomatoes

1 large carrot, peeled and cut into thick batons

1 parsnip, peeled and cut into 2–3 cm pieces

1 turnip, peeled and cut into 1-cm thick rounds

4 oz. sweet potato, peeled and cut into cubes

1 green apple, peeled, cored and cut into 8 wedges

a small handful of fresh mint leaves, roughly chopped

1⅓ cups couscous

1 tablespoon butter

sea salt and freshly ground black pepper

Serves 4

Heat the oil in a heavy-based saucepan and cook the onion and garlic over high heat for 2–3 minutes. Add all of the spices and cook for 2 minutes, until aromatic but not burning. Add 3 cups water and the tomatoes and season well with sea salt and black pepper. Bring to a boil and add the carrot and parsnip and cook over medium heat for 30 minutes. Add the turnip, sweet potato, and apple and cook for 20–30 minutes, until all the vegetables are soft, then stir in the mint.

Meanwhile, put the couscous in a large heatproof bowl with 1 tablespoon butter. Pour over 1½ cups boiling water, quickly stir once or twice, then cover with plastic wrap and leave for 15 minutes. Stir the couscous again with a fork and cover for a further 5 minutes. Finally fluff the couscous with a fork to separate as many grains as possible.

Serve the couscous with the vegetable tagine spooned over.

Next time: Try one of the couscous recipes on pages 36 or 57 to spice this meal up a bit or serve the stew in bowls with some grilled garlic flatbread on the side.

The Italians use a mixture of onions, carrots, and celery sautéed in olive oil as the base for many classic soups and casseroles. This holy trinity of veggies is known as a *soffritto* and it's right at home here in a hearty stew with sausage and beans. This is my all-time favorite dish to eat when I'm curled up in front of a movie at home.

smoky sausage and bean casserole

1 tablespoon light olive oil

12 chippolata sausages

1 garlic clove, chopped

1 leek, thinly sliced

1 carrot, diced

1 celery rib, diced

14 oz. canned chopped tomatoes

1 teaspoon Spanish smoked paprika

2 tablespoons pure maple syrup

2 sprigs of fresh thyme

14 oz. canned cannellini beans, drained and rinsed

toasted sourdough bread, to serve

a heavy-based casserole or saucepan

Serves 4

Heat the oil in a heavy-based casserole or saucepan over high heat. Add the sausages in two batches and cook them for 4–5 minutes, turning often until cooked and an even brown all over. Remove from the casserole and set aside.

Add the garlic, leek, carrot, and celery and cook for 5 minutes, stirring often. Add the tomatoes, paprika, maple syrup, thyme, beans, and 2 cups water and return the sausages to the pan.

Bring to a boil, then reduce the heat to medium and simmer for 40–45 minutes, until the sauce has thickened.

Put a slice of toasted sourdough bread on each serving plate, spoon the casserole over the top and serve.

Next time: Try replacing the sausages with 1 lb. pork neck fillet cut into 1-inch pieces. Cook the pork in batches for 4–5 minutes each batch, turning often so each piece is evenly browned. Return all the pork to the pan, as you would the sausages, and simmer for 45–50 minutes until the pork is tender.

sausages with winter rösti

I have a favorite Swiss restaurant that makes traditional potato rösti. They are crispy and hearty and served in giant wedges with snitzels or roast meats. I like to add grated celeriac to mine and thankfully it is back in fashion. There is no doubting it's a gnarly, unattractive vegetable but get over that and you will be richly rewarded. Like celery, but sweeter, it gives a base note that enhances the flavor of the other ingredients it is cooked with.

8 organic pork sausages
2 tablespoons olive oil
Dijon mustard, to serve

celeriac rösti:
3 medium potatoes, unpeeled and halved
1 small head of celeriac (about 1¾ lbs.), peeled and quartered
3 tablespoons butter
3 tablespoons olive oil
sea salt and freshly ground black pepper

Serves 4

Put the potatoes and celeriac in a saucepan and cover with cold water. Bring to a boil, then immediately remove from the heat and cover with a tight-fitting lid. Set aside for 10 minutes. Drain well and let cool completely.

Grate the potatoes and celeriac into a bowl with 1 teaspoon sea salt and some black pepper. Toss to combine. Heat half of the butter and 1 tablespoon of the oil in a large non-stick frying pan over high heat, swirling the butter around to coat the bottom of the pan. Add the potato mixture and gently press down to form a large cake. Cook for 5 minutes over high heat. Pour 1 tablespoon of olive oil around the very edge of the pan and gently shake the pan often to prevent the rösti from sticking to the bottom. Reduce the heat to medium and cook for 10 minutes, shaking the pan often.

Take a plate slightly larger than the pan. Place it on top of the pan then carefully invert the rösti onto the plate. Add the remaining oil and butter to the pan, then carefully slide the rösti back into the pan, cooked side up, and cook for 10 minutes.

Meanwhile, to cook the sausages, heat the oil in a frying pan over medium heat. Prick the sausages with a fork, add them to the pan and cook for 20 minutes, turning often, to cook an even golden brown. Spoon the rösti directly from the pan onto serving plates and serve with the sausages and a little mustard on the side.

smashed roast potatoes

It's best not to use waxy potatoes here. You will need tiny little new potatoes to make perfect smashed roast spuds. The initial blast of a really hot oven is what makes the potatoes so soft and fluffy on the inside and about to burst out of their crispy little skins. This is a novel and highly effective way to roast potatoes so be warned, it's likely you may not go back to the old way of roasting after you try this method!

16 small new potatoes (such as Nicola or chats)
2 tablespoons light olive oil
1 teaspoon sea salt

Serves 4

Preheat the oven to 450°F and put a roasting pan in the oven to heat up for 10 minutes.

Put the potatoes in a bowl with 1 tablespoon of the oil and toss to coat in the oil. Put the potatoes in the hot pan and roast in the preheated oven for 20 minutes.

Remove the pan from the oven and turn the potatoes over. Gently press down on each potato with the back of large metal spoon until you hear the potato skin pop.

Drizzle the remaining oil over the potatoes, sprinkle with the sea salt and return to the oven for a further 10 minutes, until the potatoes are crispy and golden brown.

Next time: Remove the potatoes from the oven and spoon over a soft French cheese (such as the sweet and nutty L'Edel de Cleron), while the potatoes are still warm. The cheese will melt and transform these humble roasties into a pure indulgence.

See photograph on page 148.

slow-cooked Brussels sprouts with pancetta and chestnuts

You won't be surprised to learn that Brussels sprouts (first cultivated many, many years ago in Flanders, Brussels) are a member of the cabbage family. They look just like little baby cabbages and are especially sweet, tender and tasty when they are young. Use baby sprouts in this rather festive dish, which is just as lovely on its own or as a side with roast pork, baked ham, or turkey. These are also delicious served with either the Roast Beef or Red Wine Braised Beef on page 153.

6½ oz. fresh chestnuts
¼ cup light olive oil
2 oz. pancetta, chopped into ½-inch pieces
1 small onion, finely chopped
2 garlic cloves, thinly sliced
¼ cup chicken stock
¼ cup dry white wine
1 tablespoon freshly squeezed lemon juice
14 oz. Brussels sprouts, trimmed

Serves 2

Preheat the oven to 400°F.

Cut a small slit, without cutting into the flesh, along one side of the chestnuts. Put them on a baking sheet and roast in the preheated oven for 15–20 minutes, until the skins start to split. Remove from the oven and let cool a little. Peel and rub off the skin and set aside.

Heat the oil in a heavy-based saucepan over medium heat. Add the pancetta, onion, and garlic and cook for 3–4 minutes. Pour in the stock, wine, and lemon juice and bring to a boil. Add the sprouts to the pan, cover, reduce the heat and simmer gently for 20 minutes.

Carefully turn the sprouts over and add the chestnuts to the pan. Cover and cook for a further 20 minutes, until almost all the liquid has evaporated. Serve immediately.

See photograph on page 149.

roasted pork with apple and fennel puddings

They may sound unusual but these savory puddings packed with vegetables and honey-sweet raisins make a wonderful alternative to roast vegetables.

3½ lb. pork loin roast, skin on
2 tablespoons white wine vinegar
1 tablespoon sea salt

apple and fennel puddings:
3 tablespoons butter
1 onion, chopped
1 celery rib, thinly sliced
1 green apple, grated
1 fennel bulb, grated
1 cup fresh breadcrumbs
⅓ cup raisins
1 egg, lightly beaten
1 cup chicken stock
⅓ cup flaked almonds

a medium ovenproof baking dish, lightly buttered

Serves 6

Make small incisions on the skin of the pork, ½-inch apart but don't cut through to the meat. Rub the vinegar and sea salt into the skin and set aside for 1 hour at room temperature. (This will let the skin dry out making for better crackling.)

Preheat the oven to 425°F. Put the pork on a cooking rack over a roasting pan. Pour 1 cup water into the tin and cook in the preheated oven for 30 minutes. Reduce the oven temperature to 350°F and cook for a further 1½ hours, until the pork skin is golden and crisp. Keep adding water to the roasting pan during the cooking time as necessary. Remove the pork from the oven, cover with aluminium foil and let rest for 10 minutes.

Meanwhile, make the puddings. Heat the butter in a frying pan over medium heat. When the butter is sizzling, add the onion and celery and cook for 4–5 minutes, stirring often. Add the apple and fennel and cook for 1 minute, stirring well. Remove the pan from the heat and add all the remaining ingredients, except for the almonds. Stir well. Spoon the mixture into the baking dish, sprinkle the almonds on top and cook in a preheated oven at 350°F for 1 hour. Serve slices of the pork with wedges of the fennel pudding.

roast beef with winter vegetables and garlic crème

Unlike roast pork, where the fat and skin form tasty crackling, I find excess fat on roast beef off-putting. I prefer to roast a trimmed, premium fillet and my advice is keep it lean and cook it quickly for a lovely rare roast.

1¾ lbs. beef rib-eye boneless roast
1 tablespoon freshly ground black pepper
1 bunch of baby carrots, skin left on and tops trimmed
2 small red onions, cut into thin wedges
1 turnip, cut into quarters
½ small celeriac, cut into thick batons
1 large parsnip, cut into semi circles
1 tablespoon light olive oil

garlic crème:
1 head of garlic
3 egg yolks
1 teaspoon Dijon mustard
1 teaspoon red wine vinegar
1 cup light olive oil

Serves 4

Preheat the oven to 350°F. To make the garlic crème, wrap the garlic firmly in two layers of aluminium foil and cook in the preheated oven for 40 minutes. Remove and let cool. Cut the garlic in half and squeeze the soft flesh directly into the bowl of a food processor. Add the egg yolks, mustard, and vinegar and process until smooth. With the motor running, add the olive oil in a steady stream until all the oil is incorporated. Transfer to a bowl, cover, and refrigerate until needed. Put the beef in a bowl and rub the pepper all over it. Transfer to a plate and refrigerate, uncovered, for at least 3 hours or, ideally, overnight.

When ready to cook the beef, preheat the oven to 425°F and put a baking sheet in the oven to heat up. Put the vegetables onto the baking sheet, drizzle with olive oil and roast for 30 minutes. Turn and roast for a further 10 minutes. Remove from the oven and keep warm. Heat a non-stick frying pan over high heat. When smoking hot, sear the fillet for 4 minutes, turning every minute. Put it in a roasting pan and roast in the preheated oven for 10 minutes. Turn the beef and cook for a further 5 minutes. Remove from the oven, cover with aluminium foil and let rest for 10 minutes before carving into thick slices to serve.

red wine braised beef with buttermilk mash

I give this recipe to friends who want an alternative to roasting that pays respect to premium-quality produce.

8–10 thin slices of prosciutto
1¾ lbs. beef rib-eye boneless roast
2 bottles red wine
1 onion, quartered
1 celery rib, chopped
2 bay leaves
2 tablespoons light olive oil
6 tablespoons butter, cubed
sea salt and freshly ground black pepper

buttermilk mashed potatoes:
4 large floury potatoes (such as russett), quartered
½ cup buttermilk
3 tablespoons butter
½ cup finely grated Parmesan cheese

Serves 4

Put the prosciutto slices on a flat surface, slightly overlapping along the length. Grind black pepper over the prosciutto. Place the beef along one end of the slices and firmly roll the fillet up in them. Tie with cooking twine to secure. Wrap the beef firmly in plastic wrap and refrigerate. This can be done up to a day in advance.

Put the red wine, onion, celery, and bay leaves in a saucepan large enough to take the beef fillet and bring it to a low simmer.

Heat the olive oil in a nonstick frying pan. When the oil is smoking hot, cook the beef for 4 minutes, turning every minute, until well browned all over. Add the beef to the saucepan of red wine, cover with a tight-fitting lid and simmer for 20 minutes over low heat. Remove the beef from the pan, cover with aluminium foil and let rest for 15 minutes. Strain 2 cups of the red wine mixture and put it in a small saucepan. Boil for 10 minutes then add the butter cubes, one at a time, and stir until you have a smooth sauce.

Meanwhile, put the potatoes in a large saucepan and cover with cold water. Bring to a boil and cook for 20 minutes. Drain and return to the warm pan with the buttermilk and butter. Mash well then beat with a wooden spoon until really smooth. Stir in the Parmesan and season well with sea salt and black pepper.

Thickly slice the beef and serve with the buttermilk mashed potatoes on the side and some of the red wine sauce ladled over.

chocolate orange mousse

This is an adults-only version of a classic chocolate mousse—it's very rich and slightly tipsy. The orange is God's gift to winter, its vibrant color reminding us that winter isn't as long as we think! If we can use oranges in indulgent desserts like this who cares if winter drags on!

1 teaspoon finely grated unwaxed orange zest

2 tablespoons Grand Marnier or brandy

8 oz. good-quality bittersweet chocolate (minimum 70% cocoa solids), roughly chopped

4 eggs, separated

1 cup whipping cream, whipped to soft peaks

chopped pistachios, to serve

6 individual serving dishes or wine glasses

Serves 6

Put the orange zest, Grand Marnier or brandy, and chocolate in a heatproof bowl. Set the bowl over a saucepan of simmering water for 8–10 minutes, stirring occasionally, until the chocolate has melted and the mixture becomes smooth and glossy.

Remove the bowl from the heat and let the mixture cool for 5 minutes. Whisk the egg yolks one at a time into the chocolate until smooth. Beat the egg whites until soft peaks form, being careful not to overbeat them. Fold the egg whites into the chocolate mixture in two batches, then fold through the cream until well mixed.

Spoon the mixture into 6 individual serving dishes. Cover and refrigerate for a minimum of 3 hours. Serve with the chopped pistachios sprinkled over the top.

See photograph on page 155.

baked lemon dessert

This is an old family favorite and perfect for when lemons are in abundance and inexpensive at your local market. I like to use a Meyer lemon because its thin skin and juicy pulp make it ideal for juicing and cooking. But, really, this will taste good whichever lemon you use.

3 tablespoons unsalted butter

2½ cups granulated sugar

3 eggs, separated

3 tablespoons self-rising flour

1½ cups whole milk

¼ cup freshly squeezed lemon juice

1 tablespoon confectioners' sugar

a medium ovenproof baking dish

Serves 6

Preheat the oven to 350°F.

Put the butter and sugar in a food processor and process for about 10 seconds, until smooth. Add the egg yolks one at a time to the mixture and process for a few seconds after each addition.

Add the flour and process until smooth. With the motor running pour in the milk in a slow and steady stream, scraping down the bowl of the food processer with a spatula so all the mixture is incorporated and lump free. Transfer the mixture to a large bowl.

Using a hand-held electric whisk, beat the egg whites until firm, then fold them into the batter in two batches using a large metal spoon. Quickly stir in the lemon juice. Spoon the mixture into the baking dish and bake in the preheated oven for 25–30 minutes, until golden on top.

Let the dessert rest for 10 minutes before dusting with confectioners' sugar to serve.

web sites and mail order

where to find seasonal food

www.ams.usda.gov/farmersmarkets
Farmers' markets hotline at:
1-800-384-8704
To find a farmers' market in your state, check out the list compiled by the US Department of Agriculture.

www.localharvest.org
Use this site to find farmers' markets, family farms, and other sources of sustainably grown food in your area. Includes information on where you can buy produce, grass-fed meats, and many other goodies. Features a complete A-Z listing of farmers' markets across the US.

www.csacenter.org
Provides complete information on Community Supported Agriculture (CSA) operations in your area. This is a way for the food buying public to create a relationship with a local farm and receive a weekly basket of produce. By making a financial commitment to a farm, people become "members" of the CSA.

www.foodroutes.org
Food Routes provides information about local markets, and Community Supported Agriculture farms (see above).

www.eatwellguide.org
The Eat Well Guide is a list of sustainable food resources including farms, markets, and restaurants in the US and Canada.

food markets

www.cenyc.org
CENYC, the Council on the Environment of New York City, sponsors several farmers' markets throughout the city. Visit their site for market schedules and maps.

www.williamsburgfarmersmarket.com
Historic Williamsburg hosts a hip, happening farmers market on Tuesdays and Saturdays.

www.madfarmmkt.org
The Dane County farmers' market takes place on the State Capitol Square every Saturday in Madison, Wisconsin.

home delivery and mail order

www.wholesomeharvest.com
A coalition of over 40 small family farms, all of which offer premium organic certified poultry and meats to grocers, chefs, and households.

www.localharvest.org
Over 4,500 products available to buy on-line including local produce, fruits, meats, diary, eggs, and heirloom seeds.

www.diamondorganics.com
Fresh all-organic food, with guaranteed nationwide overnight home delivery in Canada.

www.greenearthorganics.com
Organic food home delivery service with delivers pesticide free, naturally grown organic procuce

www.doortodoorganics.com
The East Coast's premier source of fresh organic produce since 1996. Delivery of farm fresh organic vegetables and fruits to your home or office.

www.wholefoodsmarket.com
Whole Foods Market is the world's largest retailer of natural and organic foods, with more than 140 stores across the US and Canada.

www.eatwild.com
Eat Wild is an excellent starting place if you're looking for sources for grass-fed beef, lamb, pork, poultry and organic dairy products.

www.seedsofchange.com
For certified organic and heirloom vegetable seeds and fruit trees available by mail order.

interesting food-related organizations

www.organicconsumers.org
Campaigning for "health, justice and sustainability." Find local food news, events, and green businesses on state pages plus information about the "buy local" movement.

www.slowfoodusa.org
Slow Food USA is a non-profit educational organization dedicated to supporting and celebrating the food traditions of North America and supporting the purity of the organic movement; from animal breeds and heirloom varieties of fruits and vegetables to handcrafted wine and beer, farmhouse cheeses, and other artisanal products.

The Monterey Bay Aquarium
This aquarium based in Monterey, California hosts the most comprehensive web site for information and resources on sustainable fisheries and "food choices for healthy oceans."
www.mbayaq.org

index

conversion charts

Weights and measures have been rounded up or down slightly to make measuring easier.

1 stick butter   8 tablespoons   125 g

Volume equivalents:

American	Metric	Imperial
1 teaspoon	5 ml	
1 tablespoon	15 ml	
¼ cup	60 ml	2 fl.oz.
⅓ cup	75 ml	2½ fl.oz.
½ cup	125 ml	4 fl.oz.
⅔ cup	150 ml	5 fl.oz. (¼ pint)
¾ cup	175 ml	6 fl.oz.
1 cup	250 ml	8 fl.oz.

Weight equivalents: / Measurements:

Imperial	Metric	Inches	Cm
1 oz.	25 g	¼ inch	5 mm
2 oz.	50 g	½ inch	1 cm
3 oz.	75 g	¾ inch	1.5 cm
4 oz.	125 g	1 inch	2.5 cm
5 oz.	150 g	2 inches	5 cm
6 oz.	175 g	3 inches	7 cm
7 oz.	200 g	4 inches	10 cm
8 oz. (½ lb.)	250 g	5 inches	12 cm
9 oz.	275 g	6 inches	15 cm
10 oz.	300 g	7 inches	18 cm
11 oz.	325 g	8 inches	20 cm
12 oz.	375 g	9 inches	23 cm
13 oz.	400 g	10 inches	25 cm
14 oz.	425 g	11 inches	28 cm
15 oz.	475 g	12 inches	30 cm
16 oz. (1 lb.)	500 g		
2 lb.	1 kg		

Oven temperatures:

110°C	(225°F)	Gas ¼
120°C	(250°F)	Gas ½
140°C	(275°F)	Gas 1
150°C	(300°F)	Gas 2
160°C	(325°F)	Gas 3
180°C	(350°F)	Gas 4
190°C	(375°F)	Gas 5
200°C	(400°F)	Gas 6
220°C	(425°F)	Gas 7
230°C	(450°F)	Gas 8
240°C	(475°F)	Gas 9